Advance

RIDE T

Journey to Peaceful Living

This upbeat testimonial will awaken you to the power within to "ride the waves" of your emotions and create your own happiness. April's ability to connect with her readers provides an inspiring platform for personal growth and insight.

~Sharon Bloom, PsyD, Licensed Psychologist

Ride the Wave has an excellent message for all who desire more peace and joy in their lives. The book provides fascinating insights into root causes of anger which so often prevent us from experiencing greater joy in life. Ride the Wave gently guides the reader from anger to an ultimate experience of the peace and joy we all desire, but so often fail to achieve. A must read!

~MICHAEL J. WOULAS, Ph.D., Psychotherapist and Author of
The Ticking Time Bomb, www.hereishelp.net

Ride the Wave is thoughtful and inspiring. This was written both for parents and teachers who struggle with managing all of their many roles and responsibilities without reacting. I felt I was guided from frustration into peace carefully and thoughtfully. Colorful examples are provided where the reader connects with the author in her struggle to find peace. I also found the exercises provided a great way to apply the concepts. This thorough program provides a wealth of realistic perspectives and the tools to teach the reader how to "ride the wave" of their emotions into peaceful living.

~SHELAGH BRODEUR, M.Ed, Middle School Educator

Ride the Wave is an absolute must read for anyone who is looking to break free from the emotional roller coaster of trying to control the outside world in order to sustain peace and happiness. April shows us how we can start the journey to a peaceful life not by changing our circumstances but by changing the way we react to any situation. If you struggle with reacting this book will definitely help you break free from it, without the need to control the outside world. With April's easy to follow steps, you can create the happiness and peace you desire right now and find that true emotional freedom is possible.

~SUE MAKOMBO, Personal Trainer and Business Owner,
www.suefitness.com

I loved this book. The stories are so personal. April writes as if she is talking directly to me. The exercises and short quizzes built right into the chapters gave me immediate and meaningful take-away tools to begin my transformations.

~TANIA MELKONIAN , Mom and Blogger,
www.ayearintheswamp.blogspot.com

April O'Leary is definitely "Riding the Wave" in her own life...a testament to her passion for making a difference, and a big one, in this world. A dedicated mom and wife, who has found a way to create the time necessary to establish herself as a woman who knows she was put here to help others find their path to life purpose, as well as inner peace.

~DAVID ESSEL, M.S., Author, "David Essel Alive"
XM 168 Positive Talk Radio Host, Master Life Coach
www.talkdavid.com

Ride the Wave is a book for all of us who are just hanging on and waiting for peace to show up at some point in the future. This book invites the reader to examine their own thought process and realize the greatness of their life—right now. April has brought practical solutions for achieving the very complicated challenge of finding peace and it's a rewarding experience for all.

~HOLLY DAVIS and BRIDGET DIRICO, Producers and Radio
Personalities for The Happy Hour Radio Show
www.thehappyhourgals.com

RIDE THE WAVE

Journey to Peaceful Living

APRIL O'LEARY

CERTIFIED LIFE COACH

ILM PUBLISHING

Printed in the United States of America

First Printing, 2012

Cover Design and Book Design by Glen Edelstein
Illustration by James Brown
Edited by Jennifer Freihoefer

ISBN-13: 978-0615548692 (Custom Universal)
ISBN-10: 0615548695

ILM Publishing
Bonita Springs, FL 34134

www.instituteforlifemanagement.com

To Mom, for always believing the best in me
and telling me so.

To Sadie, Molly and Amy for giving me opportunities to
grow in ways I never would have otherwise.

To Jim, for all we have been through and for living this
transformation with me. You are the love of my life.

I love you all and could not have written this book
without you.

Contents

Introduction

Inner peace is our piece of heaven. April has found a way to ground the sometimes ethereal quest for inner peace into real life, with real life solutions. This book doesn't demand that you escape your sometimes chaotic world to have a peaceful existence. It asks that you be present in your own life, pointing to your own heart for answers. It is inspiring to me and I hope for you. I am the co-founder of a project called "Peace Begins with Me (a small BIG peace project) dedicated to inner peace and this is a piece of the puzzle for your own inner peace project. Read it, use the tools, and you can change your life and your world! ~Joan Steffend

Joan Steffend is a national Emmy award-winning news-caster and the former host of Decorating Cents which aired on HGTV for ten years. She has appeared on Oprah, Live with Regis and Kelly, The CBS Early Show, The Today Show and Entertainment Tonight. Joan is also the author of ...and she sparkled and is the co-founder of Peace Begins With Me, a not-for-profit, humanitarian organization dedicated to education, inspiration, and collaboration in the area of inner peace. To find out more about her mission please visit www.peacebe-ginswithme.org.

By purchasing this book you are taking a first step to creating peace in the world. 10% of the proceeds go directly Peace Begins With Me.

Foreward

A few years ago I was living much differently than I am now. If you were to look from the outside you probably wouldn't notice much of a change. I am living in the same house. I am married to the same man. I am still a mother to three daughters who are growing quicker than I can believe. I still have many pets...even more than I did a few years ago! But one thing has changed. Me.

When I was newly married and had my first daughter I thought I knew what mothering was all about. Managing one baby, who had an easy disposition, was, although exhausting, doable. So I went on to have two more daughters and if that wasn't enough, I added in two kittens, a puppy and two girl guinea pigs (who ended up having two more!).

Like upping the temperature on a pressure cooker I was always on the verge of an explosion, and it was always someone else's fault. The kids were crying. The dog was barking. The house was a mess. You can add in any number of situations. Anyone and anything to blame my reactivity on would do. I would snap at the kids for the smallest infractions. I was resentful towards my husband for not helping me in the ways I thought he should. I lived in this future tense of 'when this happens...then I can be happy.' When the kids are potty trained, then it will be easier. When the house is cleaned up, then I can relax. I thought my reactions were justified. If things were different, surely I wouldn't be so overwhelmed, frustrated and angry. If things were different, then I wouldn't need to be reacting so often. To cope, I would stuff down my feelings with a drink or two during happy hour with friends and chalk it up to 'normal' mom stuff.

Seven years of pressure were building up, day upon day, week upon week, until one day I did explode. A visit from an old friend turned into more, and it could have cost me my marriage. Thankfully, through counseling, I was able to see that the real problem wasn't everyone else; it was me. I hadn't resolved my own feelings of my dad's passing ten years prior, and, on top of that, I had lost myself because I was putting everyone else first. No wonder I was so reactive.

Although I thought that others should change, I saw that the only one I was capable of changing was me. So that is what I did. I faced my unresolved emotions and started to put myself back on the priority list. By doing both of these things, the reacting that habitually hijacked my life began to subside.

Experiencing the full range of emotions is human, and I am not suggesting that I never felt anger or frustration again. There were still times when I yelled. There were still times when I said things 'in the moment of anger' to my kids, to my husband and to myself that were unkind. Although I had changed in many ways, I had not learned what to do with these feelings when they did come back. I was doing my best to keep my head above water but there were still times I felt like I was drowning.

When you were a child you probably learned how to ride a bike, swim and roller skate. You probably also learned, either directly or by example, the skills you needed to be a successful and productive woman, such as the ability to apply yourself to a project, to respect yourself and others, and to pursue life-long learning. But there is one life skill that is often overlooked because we know so little about it ourselves: how to handle negative emotions. No one ever taught us a systematic way to handle anger, disappointment, frustration or fear. Maybe right now you are thinking, "I never thought about that!" How we handle these feelings when they come up is a crap shoot, at best.

Are you like a lady I met who told me she can 'hold it in for weeks, months and even years, but when she explodes, watch out!'? Can you generally overlook things but every once in a while, snap or release your pent up emotions with a good cry and then carry on? Are you someone who resorts to consistently yelling, giving ultimatums or making vain threats? Are you someone who feels guilty for even feeling anger? Maybe you were told that it is not okay to feel these feelings, so you deny they even exist.

Let me reassure you anger, just like love, is a natural emotion that all humans experience. It is not good or bad; it is just the way we handle it that makes it so. This book will help you learn a new 'life skill' that is systematic and simple. You will be able to deal with those negative emotions in a way that will diffuse an otherwise tense situation. You will transform your view of it, from the inside out. You will learn how to metabolize your emotions by riding the wave and will then be able to objectively assess all situations by looking for the peace that can be found.

Did you know that it only takes 90 seconds from the time you are triggered for your body to flush out the chemicals it produced in that moment? The challenge is figuring out what to do during those 90 seconds. The Ride the Wave Chart will take you step by step on that 90-second journey using the acronym S.T.O.P. Each letter has an internal and an external component which describes a process of how to manage your emotions in a positive, transformative way on the inside and on the outside. I have created two charts (the visual one is in Chapter 1, and the 'cheat sheet' is in Appendix A) that show you exactly how to travel this journey. Once you know how to use the chart as described step by step, and become proficient with it, you will be able to consult it quickly and travel your 90-second journey so that you can convert anger to peace anytime, anywhere, with anyone! Riding the wave really is that easy.

Each chapter has activities to help you dive deeper into the material. Whether it is a question to answer, a quiz to take or list to complete, each one will help you personalize this system to meet your specific needs. The more you engage with this material and the more willing you are to look within through the process of journaling as described in this book, the quicker you will see results. In addition to the chapters which cover the content of the chart, there is also a chapter which addresses a common hurdle in the journey that I thought you would find helpful in crossing the bridge of ownership.

My girls have given me ample opportunities to refine this process and make it workable for the busy woman like you. And once you know it, it is something you can teach to your spouse and your children too! Molly, my middle daughter, has become so familiar with some of the material that sometimes she is the one who gives me pep talks if she sees me getting frustrated by singing a little jingle she made up, "Trigger moment…" That always makes me laugh!

This system has worked in my own life with enormous success, has eliminated my daily reacting patterns and has helped me understand myself and others like never before. I have also learned how to set tighter boundaries for myself and how to slow down in a world that is constantly prodding me to move faster and commit to more. I have used it with my clients with great success. I have spoken about it in tele-seminars and to groups as well. Through the great response, I knew it was time to get this system out to you.

Be honest with yourself. Life has brought you here, now, for a reason. Maybe you are not taking care of yourself. Maybe reacting has ruined relationships for you. Maybe you have not resolved something from your past and it is affecting your present. Maybe you just desire to live a more peaceful life where reacting doesn't create problems for you anymore. Whatever the reason, you can learn to ride the wave and experience peace in all areas of your life. It only takes 90 seconds to enjoy the journey to peaceful living!

Reminding You to Take Care of You,

April O'Leary, Life Coach
apriloleary@gmail.com
apriloleary.com

Acknowledgments

Thanking all the people who have helped me make this work possible and who have supported my efforts to write this book is a near-to-impossible task, because there have been so many of you! I will do my best.

I'd first like to thank David Essel, my mentor and friend. You have taught me in word and in deed how to be an exceptional life coach. You have been patient and kind when I had many questions and have always supported my work. I am grateful.

Thank you to all the coaches at Life Coach Universe. Our monthly Grad Nights have been most enriching and educational because of your willingness to openly share your stories and experiences. I especially thank Dr. Bill and Butch.

Dr. Michael Woulas, you have made a mark that has changed me forever. You gave me permission to take care of me at a time when I thought it was selfish. You helped me to understand what being reasonable was all about and that what I was doing – taking care of everyone else first – was unreasonable. I always looked forward to our times together, and because of you I am now able to bring this message to other women. Thank you!

Jennifer Freihofer, my editor and friend, how can I thank you enough? You came out of the woodworks to help me make this work a reality and bring it to the readers flawlessly. You have a gift, and I look forward to working together on many more projects.

Thank you, Glen Edelstein, for graciously putting up with my many design ideas and changes. You have made this book more beautiful than I had hoped, and I know the readers thank you, too.

Thanks to Steven Orsillo, friend and photographer, for helping me clarify my often-confusing message. You talked me through quite a few moments of fogginess. It is because of you that this title, Ride the Wave: Journey to Peaceful Living, was transformed from an embarrassing anger management book to a peaceful one…without the 'A.' I truly appreciate all the time you have given to me.

Sue Fit, my soul sister from afar, I am blessed to have connected with you. I look forward to our email exchanges, and I appreciate your words of encouragement as we both travel this same path together. Where will it lead us next?!

Thank you to Andrea Brezney for the opportunity to write for the Neapolitan Family Magazine and for your willingness to give me freedom to write on the topics which are nearest and dearest to my heart.

Thank you to The Happy Hour Girls, Holly Davis and Bridget DiRico, for reaching out across the often impersonal internet and picking up the phone to call me. Your kindness and support have been much appreciated, and because of you I was also connected to Joan.

Joan Steffend, what can I say? Thank you for believing

in my work and for partnering with me in our mutual mission for inner peace. I am excited, honored and humbled.

To Ginger Sauter and the entire Village School family, you have shown me love and support for my work and most importantly have given my children a place to grow and flourish. I know of no other school in the world that educates the way the Village School does. I feel so fortunate to be a part of this family and my heart is warmed every time my foot steps on campus.

Of course I have to thank all the book club girls, Teri, Jen, Irene, Karen, Maggie, Aimee, Colleen and especially Rachel and Shelagh. You have lived this book with me. Thanks for keeping me on the email list even when times were rough. Your love and support are what got me through to the other side of this journey.

To Jean O'Leary, thank you for raising such a wonderful man who is now my husband. Sometimes in the craziness of my life I step back and wonder how you did it. Your love and support through the years has been a blessing. I also want to thank Marc and Elizabeth for believing in our family.

Karen McCaw, thank you. Too many things to list, for sure, but mostly for all the long phone conversations ranging on many topics and for your support and listening ear when you could have hung up! You have been with me through thick and thin. You are more than a cousin...you are a sister in my heart. Also to Mark, Tina, Jackie and Rich...you do realize that without you I would have never met Jim, right? You are all so dear to me.

To Jim and Arlene, thank you for your constant support and help with the girls. This message of this book was born when you courageously took them to North Carolina. The first week-long break Jim and I had in ten years was nothing short of amazing, and you made it happen. I cannot thank you enough for your willingness to step in and offer a helping hand on so many occasions and for your love and support for me through everything.

Em and James, my dearest sister and brother-in-law, you two are thanked beyond measure. To Em – Thank you for giving me a childhood full of great memories and fun times, and for being not only a sister but also my best friend. Whether far or near you are always with me in my heart. James, thank you for seeing in Em all the greatness I see in her and for making her life complete. And thank you for making the illustration idea I had in my head a reality in this book. You've got skills!

To my wonderful Mom and Dad – I had to write this to both of you together; how could I do otherwise? Thank you for raising me to be sensitive to the spirit, honest and compassionate. You have taught me to see the best in others simply because you always have seen the best in me. Dad, I miss you more than I can say. Mom, I am so happy to have you near me, and thank you for being willing to take a big step to move to Florida six years ago. You bring so much joy to my life.

To my three awesome, wonderful and amazing daughters, Sadie Faith, Molly Grace and Amy Lee – You all bring such joy and laughter to my life! Sadie, I admire your ability to be a friend to everyone and your intuitiveness and sensitivity to others. You are smart, funny and kind. I love you very much. Molly, your gift for cleaning and organizing is exceptional (I wonder where you got that from?!).

You have helped me to grow up more than anyone else. I love you more than you know! Amy, my little snuggler and human blanket, you always bring a smile to my face. You have completed our family. I love you so so so so so so much.

To my constant support and life-long love, Jim – your love and support have given me the opportunity to birth this book. Not only did you have to live with me throughout these pages, you also lived with me while I got this message onto paper, and now into the world. Thank you for believing in me and sticking with me through these past eleven years. I love you more today than ever!

And to God, the most loving, most giving, never-forsaking support, thank You for speaking to me in ways that I can understand and for meeting me where I am. I trust You completely to guide me each day and I will accept the journey as it is revealed to me, knowing that You are wise beyond measure.

RIDE THE WAVE

Chapter 1

You Can Be Reaction Free

Happiness is the meaning and purpose of life,
the whole aim and end of human existence.
— Aristotle

Sarah pulls out into traffic on a busy highway, and no sooner has she hit the gas pedal but someone is on her tail, honking their horn and yelling at her. She has been up since 5 a.m. in order to have a cup of coffee alone before everyone else got up. She has so many responsibilities and frequently feels overwhelmed by it all. The irritation and anger rise up inside of her, and before she can stop herself she gives them an angry finger back.

Monica is tired and frustrated. Working full-time and being a mother is exhausting. When was the last time she had any time to herself? She can't remember. Because she is constantly running on empty she frequently snaps at her children for the smallest infractions. She wants to be the peaceful mother she has always dreamed of being but is so far from it she regrets even having kids at times. Trying to control everyone else isn't working and she is feeling more and more out-of-control. She is disillusioned and lost. "How can anyone put up with this kind of chaos?" she wonders.

Andrea smiles behind her anger. She doesn't want to let anyone know she is seething inside. She questions her feeling and doesn't want to admit that she is struggling, when everyone else around her looks so happy and satisfied. She knows she should be grateful for all she has, and that makes her feel even worse. To compensate for these emotions she enjoys her nightly happy hour, and stuffs her feelings inside. At times she finds herself quietly crying into her pillow at night. This provides temporary relief so she is able to put back on her happy face and carry on.

Heather serves her family in every way. She doesn't ask for help and is always the first to say 'yes' to others. She is the model at-home mother. Her house is always clean, her laundry perfectly folded, and she is a gracious hostess and friend. She works hard to make sure everyone else is happy, but lately she feels invisible. Other than being there to meet everyone else's needs, what is her purpose, she wonders. She feels unappreciated, taken for granted and ignored. Her resentfulness is building in her relationship with her husband, Tim, and she sees it creating a divide. They don't talk at night anymore, and she is frequently short, snappy and angry with him.

If Aristotle is right that happiness is the meaning and purpose of life, how does your life measure up? How often do moments like these interrupt your life? Do you find these feelings of agitation, frustration, exhaustion, sadness, resentment or anger surfacing in your life on a regular basis? If so, then you are in the right place!

HOW DO YOU DEAL WITH ANGER?

Each of us deals with anger in our own unique way, but there are common themes that most of us can identify with. Some of us react to the offender, like Sarah did. We get back at our inconsiderate spouse by giving them the cold shoulder. We give the rude sales clerk a piece of our mind. We feel that the provocation was enough to justify our actions. They started it, so they deserved it, didn't they?

Some of us shout to try to control what is seemingly out of control, like Monica did. We yell at the kids to get them to quiet down. We fight with our partner, thinking the loudest one will win. We are focused on trying to control the outside world and the people in it. We are frustrated because what we think should be happening is not what actually is happening. We feel temporarily better when we perceive the situation to be under control, but we carry a sense of guilt, too. Isn't there a better way than yelling to get our point across?

Like Andrea, some of us aren't comfortable with our anger. We feel that anger isn't okay. Maybe we got that message from our church or our parents, so we just submerge it. We deny it exists and hope it will go away, but we find it resurfaces through tears or a lingering feeling that something isn't right.

Or maybe we silently suffer, like Heather. We are available to others and serve them sometimes at our own expense. Yet, we find we're growing more and more resentful. How can we not be angry when we feel so unappreciated and powerless?

Looking at Sarah, Monica, Andrea and Heather, can

you see yourself? Remember, they all experienced anger but in different ways. Let's look from one other angle. What about the times when we feel angry but we don't react? How do those fit into the picture?

Many of us have our 'go-to' coping mechanisms. We turn on the television and stare mindlessly night after night. We sedate ourselves with a few drinks with friends, or alone, so we can feel better for a little while. We overeat. We try to escape by going out with friends, going on vacations, picking up new hobbies and in general trying to avoid the situations where we feel emotionally triggered. But when the cable is out, our friends have other plans, the cupboard is empty, or it rains on our vacation, anger can rear its ugly head again.

In conjunction with getting angry, or coping with anger, there are many times we react by showing power and using this power to influence people to do what we want them to do. Know that you are falling into this trap if you are:

1. Controlling others
2. Guilt Tripping others
3. Reprimanding others
4. Criticizing others
5. Showing superior knowledge or thinking you know best

Doing any of the above only further entrenches you into a reacting pattern and will create division in your relationships. If you frequently resort to this type of manipulation, know that it is not going to ultimately bring you the peace you desire.

WRITE DOWN TWO WAYS THAT YOU DEAL WITH
YOUR ANGER. HOW DO YOU USUALLY REACT?

1.

2.

For now it is enough to notice that it is normal to get angry and that the ways you deal with it are specific for you. This is what riding the wave is all about. Our emotions are the waves, but you are the ocean. Riding them is about understanding that they are always moving, always flowing, always changing. But that is just the surface of you. There is so much more underneath. If you can picture a stormy day and the rough waves crashing the shoreline, what do you suppose it is like under the surface? Calm. Quiet. Try it sometime in a pool. What happens to the noise of kids screaming nearby when you put your head under the water? You can learn to access that inner calm where you don't have to be subject to the outside conditions anymore. You can be at peace when a storm is brewing.

IT'S NOT MY FAULT

Janice had dinner ready an hour ago. It sat on the counter getting colder by the minute. The kids already ate and are almost ready for bed. This seems to her a nightly event, and she is getting sick of it. When Matt arrives home at 8:00, she is angry. She spends the evening giving him the cold shoulder, slamming the kitchen cabinets and in no uncertain terms letting him know that his behavior is unacceptable. How could she not be upset? She feels he is to blame. He is the one who is always late. She is convinced that he has no respect for her or their family and is tired of being taken for granted.

One reason we get so angry is because we feel that we are not playing any role. And it may seem like that is the case. Yet, in subtle ways we do. Take a look at a list of quotes to see if you have said any of them to your spouse or your child. Maybe you use these terms when relaying a story to a friend about how wrongly you were treated or how inconsiderate others were.

"You are making me mad."

"Don't make me get angry."

"I had no choice…"

"Why are you trying to annoy me?"

"I wouldn't have to get upset if you would stop doing that."

"They did that to me on purpose."

"Can you believe they did that?!"

"It's all your fault."

"It's out of my control."

"There was nothing I could do about it."

How does reading this list make you feel? Can you think of any others that might fall into this category? Do you notice what they all have in common? They all place the blame on someone else. They all leave us powerless to change anything, to do anything different or to accept responsibility for what is happening. These statements further reinforce our right to get angry because we think we don't have any other choice but to react how we are reacting. And many of them are so habitual that we don't even realize we are saying them.

Janice couldn't see that she was playing a role at all, so she felt justified in her anger, but she also felt powerless and stuck. It's no wonder we are getting so upset all of the time if we feel we are not part of the problem! How could we not?

INNER CALM

Can you dream of a life without reacting? Where the word 'calm' follows you wherever you go? Does it sound impossible because most of what you are reacting to seems to be out of your control? Well, there is good news. It is in your control. You have more power than you think. You have a great many choices, and the simple steps you will be shown will give you the tools you need to be able to ride the waves of your emotions.

Now that you are reading this book, maybe you see your own pattern of reacting, and you don't like it. How do you know it is a problem? It is causing hurt in your relationships. It is creating division between you and your children. It is interrupting your career success. It is causing inner turmoil and stress. It probably didn't take this book to show you that. But if you continue doing what you are doing, you will continue to get the same results. So now is the time to make a change, and it starts with you.

You don't need to berate yourself for being in the place you are right now. If you consider the fact that everyone is doing the best they can with the knowledge they have, it all makes perfect sense. You are here so that you can learn a better way to deal with your anger, and that is a great place to be.

As you read through the steps, allow yourself time to digest them. If you are having a hard time with any of the steps or feel that maybe this isn't for you, consider this idea: *How will you get different results if you are not willing to try something different?* So start with the idea of experimenting, even if only for thirty days, and withhold your judgment until then.

PUT IN THE TRAINING

Heather convinces Rick, her husband, he needs to lose some weight, so she signs him up for a local 5K race. He doesn't train. He doesn't change his diet. And he doesn't lose any weight. He shows up the morning of the event and drops out after the first mile.

How silly that would be. When someone else decides we need to change, there is often no motivation to do what is necessary to succeed. Rick would have had to acknowledge, on his own, that he needed to lose weight and then take the initiative to sign up for the race, put in the training and change his diet in order to see any results. It is all part of self-motivation. No one can do it for you.

Although it is easy to notice someone else's problems, this is stepping into the arena of 'things we can't control.'

The decision to follow this journey to peaceful living has to be about you. This is your moment. This is your chance to make a change in you. So please don't try to get everyone else on board with you right now. Yes, they may need it, but this is not about them. This is about you. Focus on you, and know that signing up for the end result – a more peaceful life – is certainly possible but will do little for you if you don't put in the training necessary.

For this program I want you to consider yourself a marathoner in training. You have 'signed up' for the race, but now you have to get up each morning and follow the plan to the best of your current abilities. Don't worry about what shape you are in now. Wherever you are starting from, each day you practice these techniques, you will build up endurance, strengthen your muscles and run with more ease. The time it takes you to create peace will begin to decrease. All you have to do is stick to the plan. Get up, do what you know to do and rest in the fact that your success is inevitable. You will soon know how to create the peace you desire in just 90 seconds.

One more word of caution: Just as a marathon runner wouldn't toe up to the starting line on her first day of training, don't expect to achieve peace on day one either. The hardest part is making the decision to commit to the plan and allowing the transformation to occur at its own pace. So lace up those shoes and let the training begin.

DIVE DEEPER THROUGH JOURNALING

I began the practice of journaling many years ago, long before I became a Life Coach. I don't remember anyone telling me to do it. It just came naturally to me. I enjoyed the process of following my train of thought, watching it unravel through my pen and onto the paper in front of me. Many times it was surprising. The ideas that I came to the table with – such as wanting to vent about a problem with a friend, or to question God about why things were happening the way they were, or to simply ask questions hoping to find an answer – often began in the vein I intended but then migrated to others topics, uncovering feelings that I didn't know lay dormant inside. That would be followed by a feeling of release, a sigh of relief and the motivation to repeat. Isn't that the purpose of journaling at any phase in life? Release. Relief. Repeat.

Maybe you want to skip this section altogether. Maybe you are thinking some variation of the following:

"I'm not the type to journal."

"I've tried that before and it didn't work."

"There's no point. It's a waste of time."

"I don't have the time."

"I don't know what I would write."

"I don't have anything to say."

If you think I have just read your mind, I did. I have heard it all before. And do you know what that is called? Resistance, (a.k.a. excuses). Let me ask you a question.

Why would you completely discount something that you have never tried whole-heartedly before? The reason resistance pops up so quickly is because it gives us an easy way out of doing the hard work. It allows us to dance around on the surface without really digging in and uncovering the real problem.

As we discuss the concept of riding the wave, journaling is the tool that you will use to bring you below the surface and explore the root cause of your reacting. It will also give you a glimpse of the calm waters that are always present, despite the size or strength of the waves above. Skipping this portion of the journey and deciding to not journal would be like traveling to the Caribbean, hiring a scuba dive instructor and then refusing to put on the tank and go below the surface. Why waste your time and money? Right?

Yes, scuba diving can be frightening, overwhelming and challenging if you have never done it before, but you can't let that initial resistance stop you. You must trust the dive instructor to guide you beyond your fear of being bitten by sharks, the idea that tank will run out of oxygen and the thought that you're going to drown. In order to see the wonders below the surface you must put on the wet suit, strap on the tank and secure the goggles. Only then will you enjoy all the beauty that scuba diving offers.

Journaling can cause the same feelings of insecurity and fear to arise. But trust me, your dive instructor, to guide you beyond your fears. Trust me to show you the value in slowing down and taking a look at the beauty that lies below the surface inside of you. Journaling will help you to see your inner thoughts and the dialogue that is hidden within. It is the best way to prevent yourself from submerging emotions (which you will learn more about later). It will help you better identify your feelings, understand where they come from, validate them and trust yourself more deeply. Do you see how much there is to gain?!

If you feel uneasy about this whole topic, that's okay. I would recommend you start by asking questions in writing and allowing yourself the space to see if the answers float to the surface. If they don't, there is no judgment, just allow yourself the freedom to sit with uncertainty. It's a great way to learn to trust life. Go slow, like you would on a first date. Be gentle and kind. Allow the skeptic to come out and 'poo poo' the whole idea if you must. There is no right or wrong way to go about it.

Most of us are guilty of treating others far above the way we treat ourselves. Through journaling you will learn how to treat yourself with kindness, love and acceptance. Remember the Golden Rule, "Do to others as you would have done unto you," but think of it in the reverse "Do to yourself as you would do to others." That version is especially important for generous and busy women. It is what I call the Platinum Rule.

Each section of the book will incorporate one journaling exercise called Dive A Little Deeper and because I am so committed to the process of journaling I am providing you with a complimentary Ride the Wave Journal. All you have to do is go to www.apriloleary.com/freejournal and download it.

THE TRANSFORMATION

Finally to tie the whole process together and to help you see that riding the wave really works, I will show "My Journey" and how I went from complete reactivity to peace, in one area of my life, without forcing the outside world to change. My goal in exposing myself is to show you first-hand how I evolved – and to give you hope that this process can work for you, too.

I chose a simple example that does not involve my relationships with anyone else (because that inevitably adds other variables), so I will focus on my dysfunctional relationship with my need to have a clean and organized house. I will take you through the same scene, adding more detail to the thought processes I faced and how they changed over time. My hope is that you will better understand what you might go through in your own transformation.

MY JOURNEY: SCREAMING AT THE STORM

I am by nature a very neat person. Systemizing, organizing and cleaning come as easily to me as making messes come to other people. As a child I loved to rearrange my room (although I didn't always keep it perfectly clean at that time). I was hired to clean houses by members of my church for extra money. To this day I frequently go through drawers, cabinets and closets to get rid of old stuff, donate to Goodwill or repurpose what I have in new ways...not because I have to, but I like to!

After having my third daughter, Amy, not only was I an at-home nursing mother, I had two other preschool-age kids home with me, too. I also had a 1-year-old puppy and two kittens...and a disastrous house! At that time, I had not learned to take care of myself first, which you will learn about in Chapter 2, and I had no idea that anything was wrong with me or my thinking. I simply didn't know there was any other way to live than how I was living.

I was in a constant state of reactivity, and the main source of my distress was stemming from a messy house. I couldn't take it. I would spend all day picking up after the girls and end up exhausted and resentful. I never took time off for myself and thought it was my duty to be the caretaker of everyone else. Normally happy and funny (at least I'd like to think so), a dark cloud parked its gloomy shadow over my head. I was overwhelmed. I would snap at the smallest mess, and I was a generally unpleasant person to be around. Yelling, snapping, blaming, criticizing and wishing things were different were part of my everyday life.

DIVE A LITTLE DEEPER

Begin right now by downloading your journal and answering the following questions. You can print it out and write it long-hand or type it.

• If I were to be honest, on a scale of 1 to 10, 10 being a lot and 1 being a little, how often does anger disrupt my life?

• Write a letter to yourself offering encouragement for where you are now.

• Set an intention starting with, "I am..." setting the goal of where you hope to be. An intention is a statement of what you want in the future phrased in the present tense. Ex. I am a calm, happy and patient woman who enjoys life.

• Post your intention on your refrigerator, write it on a notecard and put it in your wallet or place it somewhere you can read it often. Bring it to mind frequently.

A WORD OF ENCOURAGEMENT

We all start somewhere. This is where I started. But where you start is not where you have to finish. Know that life is a journey, that there is no 'finish line,' but each day you can choose to open yourself up to rediscovering the power that lies within and harness that power to change your circumstances and your life. Congratulations! You have in your hand the training manual you need to learn to ride the wave of your emotions and begin your journey to peaceful living, and it all starts with YOU! To begin your journey look at the chart on the following page and you'll see where you are headed. There is also a more detailed chart in Appendix A. Go ahead and take a peek!

Ride The Wave

Trigger · Submerged Emotions · What Is

Slow Down · People & Situations

Schedule · Emotions

90 seconds

| S | T |

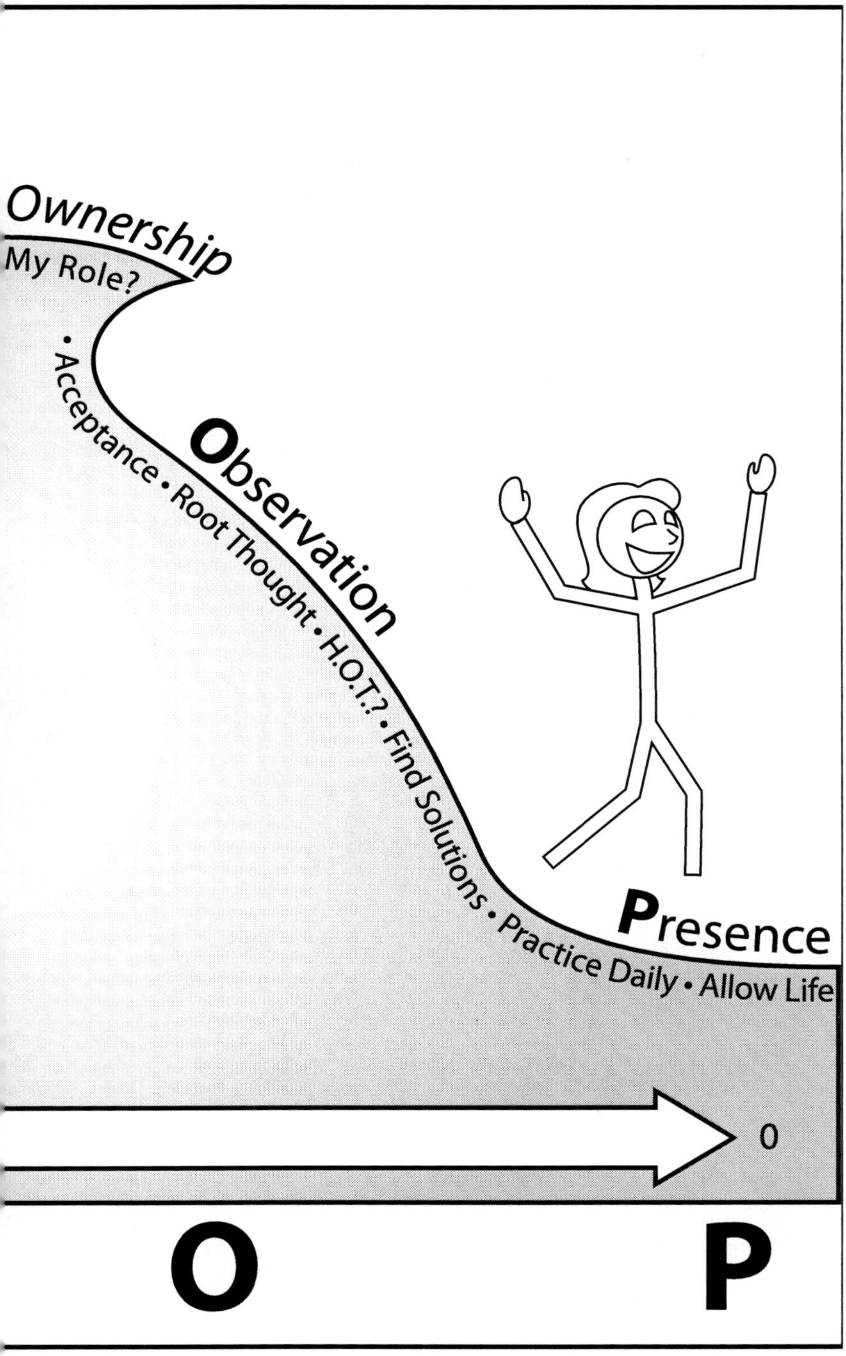
Ownership
My Role?
• Acceptance • Root Thought • H.O.T.? • Find Solutions • Practice Daily • Allow Life
Observation
Presence
0
O
P

Chapter 2

Take Care of You, First!

When you start practicing extreme self-care, a Divine force
rallies behind you to support your decision
and will actually make your life easier.
— Cheryl Richardson
Take Time for Your Life

Jennifer is rushing out of her last appointment to quickly grab the kids before school is out. She didn't get to run the errands she planned earlier because she got caught up helping a friend with her computer problems. On top of that she realizes there is a P.T.O. meeting tonight, her husband is working late and then she hears her cell phone ring. "Yes, okay. I'll be alright." The babysitter canceled, again! Pulling into the carline, Jennifer is a wreck. She has nothing in the fridge for dinner, since she didn't get to stop at the grocery like she had planned, and now she has to bring the kids back with her tonight for the meeting. What gives?! The car door opens and the kids get in. Their normal shouting and laughing are irritating. "Can't you guys be quiet for just one minute?!" she yells.

Maybe you are already thinking, "That sounds like me!" Are you constantly juggling more tasks than you can handle? Review these statements and see if any of them sound familiar. Place an 'X' next to the ones you have said before.

"My calendar is out of control."
"I have no time for myself."
"I have to do it; they need me."
"Sure, I think I can squeeze it in."
"Hurry up. You know we're already late!"

Slowing down your schedule is the first step to losing your reactivity. My goal is not to beat you up about an overflowing schedule but to help you consider the benefits and the challenges of slowing down and then guide you through specific strategies and practical tips so that you can take control of your calendar starting today. Are you ready for a little break? On your mark, get set, slow!

THE BENEFITS OF SLOWING DOWN

You wake up at 8:00 on an otherwise busy Saturday morning and check your calendar. You think to yourself, "Wait. This can't be right. There is nothing on the schedule." Then you realize, after wiping the sleep out of your eyes, you have started setting boundaries, and now you can rejuvenate with some much needed time for yourself.

How does that sound? Like a dream? Are you already saying, "That's impossible! I could never clear off my calendar to get an entire day free"? Before you bypass this section, or discount it as a pie-in-the-sky idea, remember that slowing down significantly improves your chances of living life reaction free! So don't allow that inner skeptic to discourage you. Let's back up and think of a few benefits to slowing down.

Get started now and list just five benefits that you could see immediately if you decided to start slowing down today. Don't worry about scheduling yet. Just indulge yourself. What would you be able to do that you don't have time for now? What would it feel like to not be under the emotional stress? How would it feel to not be rushing from one thing to the next? Think about the possibilities of not racing around anymore!

LIST FIVE BENEFITS TO SLOWING DOWN YOUR SCHEDULE. THINK OF EVERY AREA IN YOUR LIFE: EMOTIONAL, PHYSICAL, SPIRITUAL...

1.

2.

3.

4.

5.

Did you write down time to read a book you've wanted to read? Did you say have coffee with an old friend? Did you include time to take a nap? You could have thought of even more, couldn't you? If so, take time to write those down in the margin, too. Get motivated and see what your life could be like if you just started slowing down. How does it make you feel to consider all of the options? Can you picture yourself rejuvenated? Enjoying life more? Less stressed out?

If you didn't include "I would react less" then make sure to include it. Have you noticed the busier you are, the less patient you are and the more likely you are to snap at those around you? Living life in the fast lane is one sure way to keep you reacting because you are always running on empty.

Now that you see, on paper, the many benefits of slowing down – including scientifically proven health benefits, which you may not have even included – why don't you do it? What is holding you back? What are the reasons anyone would take on such a busy schedule? The first and most glaring one revolves around the age-old idea that to really be of service to others you must put them first!

I FEEL SELFISH TO PUT ME FIRST!

You've worked hard all week, and you are in desperate need of a break. Maybe you are an at-home mother who needs some quiet time, or a working mom who is burning the candle at both ends, wondering how much longer you can keep it up. Maybe you are a busy professional with clients who are overly needy. But in any case you just don't feel right to put your needs first. Can you relate?

Putting others needs before our own is so common, so accepted and so ingrained in our culture, especially in a woman's psyche, that it doesn't seem normal to have it any other way. Yet, look at the results: tired, angry, frustrated, worn-out, resentful people. Do you feel this way? Are you waiting for others to do for you what you could do for yourself? If this is the case, it's time to take care of you!

Slow-down Strategy #1:
START TAKING CARE OF YOU, FIRST!

Back when I was home with three children and working part-time, I was overwhelmed with kids, kids, kids. I also have the natural bent of a neat freak which didn't work so well with kids, kids, kids. So I was constantly snapping at the kids to clean up. I was aggravated that I spent so much time picking up and trying to keep the house in order only to have it get ruined again. I dreamed of having a cleaning lady, but I thought it was selfish to entertain such a wish. Wasn't that my job?

As I was sharing this story with the counselor I saw back then, I remember him asking me, "Is it reasonable that a woman with three young children and a part-time job might need help getting the house cleaned?" Bing. The light bulb went on. Of course it was reasonable!

Now that I could see that it was reasonable I had to go about hiring someone. The thoughts of guilt about the money it would cost, the feelings that I wasn't worthy of having a cleaning lady and the fears about what others would think still attacked my mind. But I kept asking myself, "Is it reasonable?" knowing that I had be okay with the idea that others might not be supportive of my decision to start taking care of me.

I had to take the necessary steps to do what I felt was right for me. So I did. Over time it became something that gave our family a lot of relief and that we all looked forward to. Additionally, getting some much-needed help alleviated a lot of needless stress for me. Overall, it has made my life more enjoyable, and it started with me making a decision to take care of me.

It is not selfish to take care of you. It is necessary. However, allowing others to help you, putting yourself and your needs back on the priority list, and changing your mindset to one of self-care first may take some time. One way to combat this is to take action. Start doing things that are a priority to you. And realize that when you start to consider your needs first, you may suffer from feelings of guilt, either internally (because you may feel you are not worth it) or externally (from others who are used to you serving them first). This is normal. But persist in it.

For example, if you are an at-home mother who would like a night out with your girlfriends but struggle with feeling guilty over leaving the children at home with your husband you can ask yourself, "Is it reasonable that an at-home mother might want a night off to go out with her friends?" Of course the answer is yes. So if this is the case, do it – despite lingering guilty feelings or the fact that at first your husband might not be so supportive – knowing that what you are doing is reasonable.

If you are working and have children and somehow carry the load of full-time mother too, you might have to talk with your family about sharing more of the at-home responsibilities. The kids might need to start helping cook meals. Your spouse might have to start helping with the laundry. If this is not possible you might have to consider hiring outside help. It is not reasonable to do it all yourself and you might have to stop feeling guilty if you can't do it all.

If you are a business owner and you start setting boundaries so that you are not as available to your clients night and day as you were formerly, you might find that others aren't so happy about it. This is also okay. Doing what you need to do to take care of you first is perfectly normal, healthy and acceptable.

Additionally, the more you allow others to help you, the more you are giving them an opportunity to use their gifts and to feel good about serving (just like you do when you serve others). I had one client who was struggling with the idea of getting help with organizing her house. But once she saw that by hiring help she would be allowing someone to use their talents, the decision became much easier. They could do in a few hours what might take her an entire weekend to do. We are all interconnected and need one another. If you have a specialty as a tax accountant wouldn't it seem reasonable that someone who has no knowledge or interest in taxes would hire you to help them? Of course! You don't have to know how to do it all, nor do you have to feel guilty if you can't do it all! Let others serve you with their expertise in the way that you would be happy to serve others.

If you struggle with this concept of putting your needs first because your background, religion or culture has taught you otherwise, please go to the following link to hear a short tele-seminar that may clear up a bit of confusion: *www.apriloleary.com/freeseminar.*

To sum it up putting yourself first is not selfish also long as you do what you feel is reasonable for you. Get help in the areas you need help. Realize that feelings of guilt surrounding putting yourself first are normal, but don't give in. Over time, those unreasonable feelings will vanish and be replaced with a feeling of relief.

IT'S NOT MY JOB TO PLEASE OTHERS

Grace had not had a day to herself, as best she could remember, in over a month. She was tired and frustrated but seemed to be able to keep running on empty. On top of working full-time and juggling two children, her husband, Tom, was never around. He was too busy and stressed-out with his own career and was depressed most of the time he was home. She frequently made meals that he liked, picked up around the house, did the laundry and tried to lighten his load, only to feel he didn't appreciate, or even notice, her efforts. Grace tried desperately to get his attention, and to make him happy, but couldn't. "What am I doing wrong?" she wondered.

What is she doing wrong? I bet the answer would surprise you. Grace is making it her job to make Tom happy. But what she doesn't realize is that it is not her job to please Tom or to make him happy. That is outside of the realm of what Grace can control. Grace needs to slow down, take care of her needs and release the need to please her husband or make him happy.

Slow-down Strategy #2:
RELEASE THE NEED TO PLEASE OTHERS.

There is a story told by Jerry Hicks in the book *The Astonishing Power of Emotions* that I believe is an excellent illustration of this concept. Paraphrased, it is about a man who loves to golf. He loves his wife, too, who hates his golfing habit. Every time he goes out golfing she gets upset. So giving in to her constant nagging, he quits golfing to make her happy and decides to spend more time with her. He accompanies her shopping and does things with her that she likes to do. Now she is happy! But he is slowly becoming more and more unhappy. He gave up what he loves to do in order to please someone else, namely his wife.

So now that he is unhappy, he is no longer a good companion for his wife. She places more demands on him, blaming her own unhappiness on his foul mood. Now they are both unhappy. What are they to do?! Hicks suggests that, in order to help others find happiness, the best thing you can do is remain happy.

Do what makes you happy, and others will follow your lead. If this man decided to continue golfing and remain happy, his wife would have to either remain miserable or find a way to make herself happy. She could invite a friend out to coffee, join an exercise class, learn how to paint or volunteer at the school, but the only responsibility her husband has in relation to her happiness is to continue doing what makes him happy.

Let me ask you a few questions. Have you ever done something just to keep the peace? Have you ever sacrificed what you wanted in order to make someone else happy? How did it make you feel when you realized your efforts weren't working? Angry? Resentful? Powerless? The more we try to make others happy, the more they depend on us to make them happy. Don't you see that this is a losing battle? Each person is responsible for his or her own happiness.

Does that make sense? I hope so. You can never 'make' someone else happy by modifying your life. That is out of your control. So focus on what is in your control: you.

And then you will see that as you remain happy, others around you will be forced to find their own happiness, too.

IT'S OKAY TO SAY 'NO'

Many years ago I was the president of our local MOMS Club. Sadie and Molly were 3 ½ and 2, and although I was supposedly an at-home mother, I was never 'at home.' I was constantly running from one activity to the next. On top of caring for two toddlers, I had said 'yes' to this position because no one else was stepping up to the plate. Of the 80 members in the club, many went to the playgroups, but only a handful were participating in the fundraising events, only a few showed up at the monthly meetings and only a half dozen were truly committed to helping me run the club.

I remember one meeting I hosted for which I sent out invitations, bought donuts and coffee, created an activity for the kids to do while the moms met, and contacted a local parenting magazine to come take photos and cover our meeting to promote our club...and do you know what, not one member other than me showed up except the magazine editors who graciously laughed with me about the lack of attendance.

But I was resentful. I didn't realize that I chose to be the president by saying 'yes.' I felt it was my job, and I was getting more and more frustrated. What was once a fun playgroup for my kids and a social outing for me had become more of a responsibility and burden.

Slow-down Strategy #3:
DON'T BE AFRAID TO SAY 'NO.'

Why did I say 'yes'? Looking back I can see that I had a need for approval. I wanted to be liked. I didn't think of myself first, or at all. I thought of everyone else but me. And then when no one seemed to care how much work I was doing, or bothered to show up at the meetings, I became frustrated and angry. I was doing things just to be accepted, yet no one seemed to care.

How often do we do this to ourselves? We say 'yes' when we really want to say 'no.' We fear what others will think if we say 'no,' or we feel that without our help, support or time, these groups, organizations, charities and people wouldn't succeed. Is that really the case? Had I not said 'yes' to being the president that year, would the club have folded? I don't think so. As far as I know it is still going strong to this day.

Another way to look at this is when we say 'no' we are opening up the opportunity for someone else to say 'yes.' For those of us in the 10% of people who consistently volunteer for every group, who are on every board and who have no time, maybe the real problem is that we are so quick to say 'yes' that we are not giving the other 90% of people (who may take a little longer to decide) and opportunity to say 'yes' and to use their gifts and talents to serve. If you can consider this the next time you are asked to join one more activity it might be easier to slow down and say 'no.'

Slow-down Strategy #4:
NEVER SAY 'YES' ON THE SPOT.

One more tip on this topic: Never say 'yes' on the spot. I have found that it is always a good practice to give yourself some time to think before committing to anything. Memorize this statement if you must: *"Thank you for the opportunity. I appreciate it! I need to check my calendar, and I will get back with you tomorrow."* Even if you have your calendar with you, do not consult it then! Go home and think about what the proposed commitment would entail.

Questions to consider before saying 'yes':

- How much time would I need to give?
- Do I have that time available?
- Am I interested in this activity?
- If I said 'yes' would I be excited to go when the time came?
- Do I feel this opportunity fits with my specific gifts/talents?
- Am I afraid that if I said 'no' this person or committee wouldn't understand?
- Do I feel like I don't have a good enough excuse to say no?

Check in with your feelings and learn to trust them. Never make a decision that is based off of fear or obligation or if it creates added stress. Your feelings are a very accurate guide and you must learn to trust them. If after answering these questions and giving yourself a gut check, you decide you do not want to participate simply contact that person and tell them. You may also want to memorize this statement: *"Thank you for the opportunity. I have looked at my calendar, and this is not going to work for me at this time, but I appreciate you thinking of me. Good luck!"* Don't leave room for negotiation and feel confident in your quality decision.

I had a client, Mindy, who used this strategy with great success. She was always over-booked and stressed out. She regularly put others' needs before her own. Through our work together she realized that the reason she was living life in a frenzied state was that she was the one who was committing to too many activities. Once the light bulb went on and she gave herself permission to say 'no,' she was given yet another opportunity to commit.

Someone approached Mindy to head up the Toys for Tots toy drive one Christmas for her church. The *old* Mindy would have said 'yes' without giving it too much thought and regretted it later. The *new* Mindy was able to slow down, give herself time to think and review the questions above. She ultimately decided she didn't have the time to commit and felt a huge sigh of relief in calling the coordinator and telling them 'no,' To rectify the solution in her mind she agreed to donate a toy instead. By her courageous decision to say 'no' she also paved the way for someone else to head up that project who would truly be blessed to serve. Way to go, Mindy!

SETTING BOUNDARIES

Jennifer is a full-time working single mother and is the president of the school P.T.O. Rachel owns her own marketing company, volunteers at the local homeless shelter and is on her neighborhood board association. Tara is an attorney in a high-volume law firm and is expected to bill more hours than she has in a day. On top of that, she has two young children and a husband who want to see her sometimes, too. What do Jennifer, Rachel and Tara have in common? They are all over-committed, exhausted and edgy.

If you looked at any of their calendars they probably wouldn't look too different from yours. Am I right? Whether an at-home or working mother, or a busy woman without children, the struggles we face are similar. Most of us are over-scheduled. If your calendar is overflowing and you feel angry, resentful, tired and stressed-out most of the time, you need to reassess your boundaries. Saying 'no' is a great start, but now we can take it one step further. And look at the practical side of setting boundaries for ourselves from here on out.

How can someone start setting boundaries? What does that mean? Setting boundaries means that you know what you will and won't do. It means that you have decided ahead of time what is important to you and what you want your schedule to look like and you stick to it, come hell or high water. Does that sound reasonable? It is. But first *you have to know you.*

Slow-down Strategy #5:
KNOW YOURSELF AND SET YOUR BOUNDARIES.

Now that you are in a relaxed state, I hope, let's take a look at your schedule. How do you feel when you look at your calendar for the upcoming week? Are you excited about it? Or do you have a feeling of dread? Are there certain activities that you have committed to that you just don't enjoy anymore? Are there things that you are doing just because you feel obligated to do it? Just because you have done something in the past does not mean you have to continue doing it in the future.

Since this book is about learning how to create peace in your life, we are focusing on slowing down for the sheer benefit of helping to alleviate much of your re-acting. One of the quickest ways we contribute to our reactivity is that we deplete our energy reserves before we have even had the chance to replenish them. With-out setting boundaries we are more prone to reacting because we carry with us the feeling that life is not fair. We feel that everyone else is getting their needs met, and we think that no one is doing anything for us. We wonder when we will get a break, yet we see no break in sight! Soon enough that trapped feeling sets in, and the reactions begin.

Complete this next activity to help you decide where you want to set your boundaries. The answers will be specific to you. There are no right or wrong answers here. This is only about what you feel is reasonable for you.

HOW MUCH TIME WOULD YOU LIKE FOR YOURSELF? DO NOT CONSIDER WHAT YOU CURRENTLY HAVE, WHAT OTHERS WOULD THINK OR IF IT IS EVEN POSSIBLE. IN YOUR IDEAL WORLD, HOW MUCH FREE TIME WOULD YOU HAVE (IN MINUTES, HOURS OR DAYS)?

I WOULD LIKE TO HAVE:

_____ EACH DAY.

_____ EACH WEEK.

_____ EACH MONTH.

Now look at your calendar and schedule in that time. If you think this is an impossible task with your current schedule, you might be right. That is where some cut-throat elimination will take place. Get ready! Go find your calendar and look at the list of things you have to do. As I said earlier, I love to systemize, so here is the plan. What I am asking you to do is similar in nature to the show *Clean Sweep* on HGTV where they make the participant put their junk into three piles on the front yard: keep, sell and toss. Be objective. Sort quickly. Don't give it too much thought by considering how you would cut those things out. That will come later. For now just an overall assessment is best. Be generous with the 'could cut out or delegate' group!

GET OUT YOUR CALENDAR AND CATEGORIZE YOUR SCHEDULE. WRITE OUT YOUR DAILY, WEEKLY AND MONTHLY ACTIVITIES INTO THREE CATEGORIES: MUST DO, UNDECIDED, COULD CUT OUT OR DELEGATE.

Great! Now that you have your list, review it. What else could you move from 'must do' over to 'undecided'? What could you move from 'undecided' over to 'could cut out or delegate'? Remember our roadblocks to slowing down – not putting ourselves first, the need to please others and the inability to say 'no'? Are any of these reasons why you are not able to move some of these activities into the 'could cut out' list? If they are, realize that this new way of living will not please everyone, but it will make us happier and by being happy we pave the way for others to be happy too. It just takes practice. So here is the final activity to slowing down.

WHAT ARE YOU GOING TO DO TODAY TO ELIMINATE ONE OF YOUR 'COULD CUT OUT OR DELEGATE' ACTIVITIES? BE SPECIFIC. WHO DO YOU NEED TO SPEAK WITH? WHAT ARE YOU GOING TO SAY? WRITE YOUR ANSWER BELOW.

Have you ever had a boss who had a hard time delegating or if they gave you a job stood over your shoulder and micro-managed it? When someone manages in this way it creates employees who are unsure of themselves, who can't make decisions and it places unnecessary strain on the manager. Consider yourself the household manager. Do not make it your job to run the house single-handedly, even if you are an at-home mother. You are not the only one who lives there, if you have a family, and everyone should learn to pick up their things, put them away and participate in routine jobs and errands.

One of the easiest and most cost-effective ways to slow down is to delegate. Many times we are simply doing for others what they could and should be doing for themselves. Including our children! I have long been a subscriber to creating independent children, and because they are so capable it often surprises others. Even as young as four a child can get a drink for themselves. I suggest that if they ask you to do it, don't. When faced with a complaint of, "I'm thirsty!" respond with a question, not a glass of water. Ask them, "What could someone do who is thirsty?" Let them come up with a solution and then take action on it. This will empower them to meet their own needs and will alleviate you from being needed by all.

Strike when the iron is hot. Recall the feelings you tapped into at the beginning of this chapter and the things you'd like to do when you finally have the time to do them. Don't allow the fear of rejection or the need for approval or any of those other roadblocks stand in your way. Realize there will be an adjustment period. But ultimately it is your life to live it as you choose. So if you choose to slow down, do it! Knowing that the benefits surely outweigh the temporary discomfort of reassigning chores, asking for help from others or making a phone call to tell someone, "I'm sorry I can no longer participate, but I wish you all the best."

MY JOURNEY: A FIRST STEP

What was my first step? In Chapter 1 I told you about my own challenges with being home and overwhelmed, how reacting had become the norm for me and how much of it stemmed from my inability to keep the house as neat as I thought it should be. I should also mention to you that I was not always so stressed-out. As a single woman I was very busy too, but I did not struggle with yelling and anger like I was experiencing now that I had three children. I was confused at this behavior and hated the person I had become. But I did not know how to stop myself.

By year eight of parenting, I was a mess. The full-time, around-the-clock schedule had taken its toll. Although Sadie and Molly were in full-time school, I still had Amy at-home with me. In addition, I was working part-time as a four-year old teacher. This was not a good fit for me and it just complicated my already child-filled life. For relief, I was having my own happy hour each day, with or without friends, so I could try to escape what was inescapable.

After ending a brief emotional affair with an old friend I had reconnect with through Facebook, I received some much-needed counseling. Through it I realized that the problem wasn't everyone else; it was me. I was putting everyone else first. I felt guilty if I did anything for me. I was stuck in the trap of trying to please others and had lost myself in the process. I was trying desperately to make everyone else happy, and when they weren't, I wondered what I had done wrong. I hadn't set boundaries for myself, and I was letting everyone else's agendas dictate my time and their moods affect my emotions.

At this point, I learned to start asking myself the question, "Is it reasonable?" about everything. That little technique helped me begin to release the feelings of guilt that plagued me when I was doing something that I enjoyed or when I was taking a break from the kids.

I also hired some help with the housekeeping by answering the question, "Is it reasonable that someone with three young children might need help with the housework?" The feelings of guilt over doing this persisted, though. I cringed when I wrote them a check and had a hard time feeling I was worth it. I can remember not wanting anyone to think I couldn't handle it all or that I was princess-y.

Little by little, things started to turn around. Like a ship changing courses, these small adjustments to my thoughts and actions made a world of difference. I felt relief. I regained my sense of self. I was no longer defining myself in relation to others but was able to see what I wanted and slowly take steps to overcome my unhealthy guilt that was preventing me from taking care of myself.

However, I still had my ups and downs with the house situation. I was happy when the house was clean. But I was frequently still upset when it was messy. I would be irritated, frustrated and outright angry when the clean house only lasted for 24 hours. I had broken free from pleasing others, a little bit, but was still in the trap of allowing the outside world to dictate my moods. I didn't know there was any other way to live. I still didn't realize that the trigger was not coming from the messy house but from inside me.

DIVE A LITTLE DEEPER

Now that you have learned the ways in which you can slow down on the outside and the specific strategies that you can implement to start setting boundaries in your day-to-day life, it's time to do a little digging. Look back at the calendar activity and reassess each activity you listed. Tap into your feelings. Answer the following questions in your journal:

- Why do I consistently over-commit myself?
- Why am I afraid to say 'no'?
- What can I do to start clearing off my schedule, and do I really want to make a change?
- What is holding me back from taking care of myself first?

Many times when I journal I find that I end my sessions with a question or a lingering thought that is unanswered. Doing that is a great way to keep yourself open and thinking about the bigger ideas you want to find answers to. Allow yourself the pleasure of not knowing.

If you find you are not able to effectively set boundaries, if you feel inhibited by an overwhelming sense of guilt in taking care of yourself first, or if you are afraid to take the steps necessary because of the reactions you may get from those around you, I would encourage you to go to *www.instituteforlifemanagement.com* and get the home study course called Focus On You: Your Needs Matter Too. It was created to help you identify healthy and unhealthy forms of guilt and fear and give you simple techniques that you can use to overcome them so you are better able to take the steps I have outlined in this chapter.

A WORD OF ENCOURAGEMENT

Slowing down on the outside is the first step to losing re-activity. If you are constantly rushed, over-booked and ex-hausted, you cannot possibly expect to live in peace. And that is the goal, right?

Start today by making small changes to eliminate the things on your calendar that you no longer enjoy or that someone else could do. Challenge yourself to create a schedule where your 'desired' amount of daily, weekly and monthly free time becomes a reality for you. Delegate gen-erously. As you start to slow down, release the idea that it is your job to please others and put your needs back on top of your priority list. You will find by doing so that much of the habitual reacting that hijacks your peace and the feel-ings of resentment towards others will subside.

Take it slow. You don't have hit the brakes with full force; just a gentle tap will do. Pick one of the above strat-egies and begin working on it over the next seven days. Figure out how you can start to put yourself back on the priority list and release the need to please others. If you make the commitment to take one baby step each day, you will soon notice how simple it is and how peaceful life can be. I give you permission to start taking care of you today. This completes the first step of the journey: S is for Slow Down Your Schedule.

Chapter 3

Ride the Wave

*We know that when anger is present in us we should refrain
from reacting, namely from speaking, or doing anything.*
— Thich Nhat Hanh

Slowing down your schedule is such an important part of
the journey but in addition to slowing down on the outside, you must also learn how to slow down on the inside.
What does that mean? It is taking the advice of Thich Nhat
Han and doing nothing when anger is present in you. You
are simply recognizing your feelings in whatever form they
arrive and allowing them to exist within you without reacting to them. It can be likened to standing on the shoreline
and watching the waves of the ocean rise and fall, without
commenting on each one as it does what it is meant to do.

THE NATURE OF WAVES

Picture yourself on a beach. You are walking slowly
looking out over the ocean. Your feet are gently stepping
on the wet sand. As you watch the waves break, cover-
ing the beach with their salty water and retreating again,

what are the words you would use to describe them? Flowing? Rising? Rough? Smooth? Cold? Warm? Refreshing? Graceful? Strong? However you might describe the waves today is subject to change. Tomorrow, or one hour from now, they might be totally different so a great description for waves is 'always changing.'

What causes the waves on the surface? What keeps them moving and determines their size and strength? I wondered that myself, and although the answer might seem fairly obvious to some, I decided to go about this very scientifically, through a little internet research. The simplest answer I could find was that the force and the speed of the wind determines the size of the waves. That seemed to make a lot of sense to me, and for our journey in learning to ride the wave, it applies perfectly.

We can think of the relationship between the wind and the waves in two ways. If you go to the beach on a windy day, the waves will be large and rough. If there is little wind, and the skies are clear and sunny, the waves will be smooth. In the Gulf of Mexico the water can come to an almost still, glass-like appearance during these times. But, if a hurricane is looming, watch out! Let's dive a little deeper into this analysis.

Can the ocean create its waves? That may be a silly question, but I am going somewhere with this line of thinking, so humor me. Is the ocean responsible for its own waves? Certainly not. The wind is the controlling factor. Right? Here are other questions to consider: Does the ocean have the ability to control the wind? Does the weather man? Do you? The wind blows as it will, and where it stops nobody knows. Although invisible the wind is a powerful force that moves even the waters of the vast ocean. It is one factor that cannot be controlled by anyone or anything. It is what it is. The ocean simply responds to it.

There is another more predictable quality of the ocean: the tides. The tides depend on a number of factors. According to Wikipedia they are determined by the gravitational pull of the sun and the moon along with the centrifugal forces generated by the earth's rotation. We all probably learned that somewhere along the way. People who enjoy boating use predictable tide tables to plan out their course. I don't boat, but I do consult the tide charts to determine the best time to bring our playful Labradoodle Barkley to the dog beach, because no one wants to visit the doggy beach at high tide...trust me! Although tides are predictable, like the waves they are always changing, too.

This is obviously not rocket science, but noticing nature can give us clues to our inner world. So what are the hidden clues? What messages can we uncover from the predictable tides and the ever-changing patterns of the waves? Open yourself up to the possibilities of noticing parallels. Just by asking questions we can start to uncover some truths that we have known all our lives but never took the time to really see before.

THE NATURE OF EMOTIONS

Let's answer some of these questions. How are we like the ocean? What can we uncover about our emotions by looking at the way waves are created? How do the tides parallel predictable patterns in our emotions? Stick with me here and really think about it. The wind is life, the outer situations and experiences that 'happen' to us each day. It is the invisible force that is uncontrollable by anyone. Arguably we have some power over some of these situations which can be manipulated, created and such, but ultimately life has a will and power of its own that we cannot consistently control.

We are the ocean. We have great mysteries inside of us. We are vast and powerful. There are many hidden mysteries that have yet to be discovered inside of us. We possess an inner peace and beauty that can only be seen by going below the surface. Did you know the highest mountain in the world is actually under the ocean?!

Our emotions are the waves and tides of the ocean. Like the tides our moods can rise and fall in predictable patterns. Each month most of us go through predictable PMS patterns that I'll call 'high tide'. By noticing these predictable patterns though, we can plan accordingly. We can slow down and take better care of ourselves during these times. We can avoid 'saying or doing anything' that would create contention unnecessarily. For many women this time of the month can be very intense, and for others not significant at all. You know which category applies to you. Don't fight the tides. Accept that high tide comes, but take heart in the fact that it will give way to low tide soon enough.

Our emotions, like the waves, can also be affected by the strength and force of the wind, which are life's circumstances. Can you see that in yourself? When the winds of life are blowing change through your life or when unpredictable things happen that are out of your control, do the emotions you experience get stronger? This is true for 'windy' life events, both positive and negative.

Think about a time in life when you experienced a lot of positive change. Maybe you graduated college, got a big promotion, got married, bought a pet, or had a child. These windy times of change probably evoked strong positive emotions of love, excitement and passion unlike those you experience on a regular basis.

Now consider a time when you experienced a lot of negative change. Maybe you got a divorce, lost a job, foreclosed on your house or experienced the death of a parent, spouse or child. How did the winds of life affect your emotions then? Were you deeply angry, depressed, frustrated or despondent? Were you more likely to fight with others, lash out or cry? If you are human, you probably did one or all of these things. Again, were these events in your control? Not completely. Did your emotions respond? Yes. Noticing both the positive and negative winds of change is essential to your ability to accept the nature of emotions and how they are influenced by invisible forces outside of your control.

It is also important to recognize that there are times when the wind is calm. Life is smooth and carries on day after day without so much as a ripple. In these times your emotions are most likely stable. You don't experience your highest highs, but you also don't experience your lowest lows. Waves and tides are not good or bad; they are just two qualities of the larger ocean, which is you.

The winds and tides are created by forces of their own. Can you ultimately control or stop them or still their effects on the ocean? No. But, does the strength of the wind, the predictable tides or the height and strength of the waves change the ocean as a whole? No. Here is another deeper thought. Are the fish concerned about the waves above? No. Like the fish in their underwater habitat are unaffected by the waves above, when you live more deeply, in a state of inner peace, you are not affected by the waves of your emotions or the outside circumstances of life either. Have you ever thought of that? I would like to suggest that only those above the surface are affected by the wind and the waves…those below the surface don't even notice them.

The waves are not what define an ocean, just as your emotions are not what define you. They are only the topmost layer of you, the thing that others most often see and experience. But there is so much more below the surface of you that you can't even see yet. Through this process you will discover that the peace you want comes not from trying to change the outside world or control it, but by letting go of your need to react on your ever changing circumstances and emotions and making a commitment to go below the surface and access the peace that is always present within you.

Realize that your emotions are forever changing. They rise and fall. They are sometimes strong and other times calm. This is normal. But understanding that there is far more peace and stability below the surface will help you realize that reacting to every wave of emotion is not as important as you once may have thought. It is exhausting at best and debilitating at worst.

Just like the waves will pass when the wind changes, and the tides will fluctuate, so will your emotions. Standing on the shore and shouting at the waves to calm down would be ridiculous, and getting frustrated for feeling the way you feel is equally as ridiculous. Emotions come and go. The only thing that can be done when they are rising is to watch them and wait. Soon enough they will retreat again, like they always do.

When you detect anger or frustration rising up within you, what can you do? Slow down for just 90 seconds. That is all it takes. Allow it space to exist in its natural state, without resisting or reacting to it. Just stand there and watch. Breathe. By not reacting you will be able to implement the rest of the Ride the Wave plan during those 90 seconds which we will continue to explore in detail.

BELOW THE SURFACE

At times when I go to the beach and step my foot into the cloudy water, I feel a bit nervous. The nagging thoughts that plague me go something like this: "What's under there? Is a shark nearby? Am I going to step on a crab?" These ideas try to prevent me from having a good time on an otherwise beautiful occasion. Stepping on a sharp shell further solidifies the thought that "I'm not safe in here."

I discussed this with a friend as we sat on beach chairs one day, watching our children play in the sand and swim in the ocean without a care in the world, and she too felt the same way. Then she went on to tell me that, although apprehensive about walking in the murky shallow waters of the Gulf of Mexico, she loved scuba diving. She described a recent trip she took to the Florida Keys with her husband.

She raved about the beautiful colors and the diverse sea life she saw. I asked her with curiosity, "Aren't you afraid that something will bite you?" She said, "No, because I can see everything." Bingo. The light went on for me.

This is what riding the wave is all about. It is one thing to be able to notice the waves and the tides and to allow them to rise and fall. But there is still a certain amount of apprehension or fear that needs to be dispelled. If we are afraid of what is inside of us, we will remain hesitant to truly take the plunge and dive under the waters to explore our inner world. This is the reason we first have to slow down. We have to give ourselves enough time and space to go deeper and explore below the surface so that we can truly see the beauty and stillness that is there. Our emotions are a gift, an invitation to go below the surface and explore what is hidden below. The fear will subside when you do because you'll be able to see what is around you. This process of seeing within ourselves will come later when we start to observe the root causes of why we react in Chapter 8. For now it is enough to know that, by not reacting to the wind and the waves, you will create the space you need to keep going down the path to peaceful living. And rest assured, there is nothing to fear!

RIDING THE WAVE OF EMOTIONS

Many of us are familiar with or have tried some basic anger-management strategies such as counting to ten or removing ourselves from the situation. These strategies are certainly helpful at this stage and you can use them when you need to slow down your emotions so that you don't react on the spot. Taking a moment to slow down your thoughts and emotions when you are starting to feel triggered is always wise.

Slow-down Strategy #6:
SLOW DOWN YOUR EMOTIONS.

This is the one we will focus on for the rest of the book. It is certainly important to slow down your schedule in order to give yourself a chance to learn how to manage your emotions in a way that will be more productive and peaceful overall. But from here on out we will be talking specifically about times when emotions come back with a force and how to handle them when they do. Because you are human, there will be times that this is the case. As I shared at the opening of this book, riding the wave is not about learning how to eliminate negative emotions it is about how to handle them productively and systematically when they are crashing on the surface of your ocean. That is when the S.T.O.P. strategy can take over…all you need to do is get on and ride the wave.

BUT I'M FACING A TSUNAMI!

How many of us remember what we were doing on December 26, 2004? I have a vague idea that I was taking down my Christmas tree, cleaning up after a large family party, gorging myself on leftovers all while watching two toddlers. But while I did that, another part of the world experienced a great devastation: the Sumatra Tsunami.

Approximately 150 kilometers off the west coast of northern Sumatra in Indonesia, the greatest earthquake in 40 years took place. It was a devastating natural disaster that caused destruction in eleven countries bordering the Indian Ocean. It is thought that waves may have reached a height of eighty feet and killed nearly 300,000 people. The aftershocks were felt by many and lasted a full week afterwards. What is the point of sharing this with you?

Since we are trying to draw references to our own emotions using the wisdom of nature, I'd like to talk for a minute about the tsunamis of life. You have probably experienced at least one earthquake that caused a life-sized tsunami. Maybe it was finding out your spouse wasn't faithful, getting fired from a job for something you didn't do or getting breast cancer. Of course those unpredictable events did a great bit of damage to your emotions and no doubt caused enormous waves to come rolling onto shore. So what can this story about the Sumatra Tsunami teach us? That is a great question!

Seemingly, certain events in life are out of our control. No force of human effort, pre-planning or foreknowledge could have prevented two underwater tectonic plates from slipping and causing a huge tidal wave that December. In life, there are also events that are not controllable. No amount of planning, predicting or preparing can strop certain catastrophes from coming our way. Whatever your life tsunami is, the emotions that come during those times and the after-effects you experience are normal and natural. But within this story, there is another layer underneath; a lesser-told story, but a fact nonetheless.

Would it surprise you to know that at the time of this tsunami, there were two Americans scuba diving in the Indian Ocean off the coast of Ko Phi Phi Island? Would it also surprise you to know that they were completely oblivious to the enormous wave that roared up above them? According to a CNN report Faye Wachs, 34, was diving with her husband, Eugene Kim, when they noticed the clarity of the water worsened. The dive master signaled for them to surface, and even he didn't know what had happened until receiving a text message from his wife telling him about the tsunami.

Wow! Think about that for a minute! What does this say to you? Can you draw a parallel between the tsunamis of life and this story? How could someone be enjoying a dive when a catastrophe roared up above their heads and caused destruction, death and devastation for many thousands of people? How could they remain unharmed and unaware?

I know this may seem like a far stretch. Is it really possible to be able to experience a tsunami without realizing it or being affected by it? This is a factual story, and the point I would like to make is that it seems it is possible. I didn't say the tsunami didn't affect countless thousands of others. I did not say that it did not create a ton of surface damage and destruction. It did. But for these three individuals, the story was different. Could it be different for you? Can you go deep enough below the surface, within yourself, to access the peace that is within you, where the destructive waves above don't affect you? Can you learn to ride out the disaster while remaining at peace unlike those around you? What I am doing by drawing this analogy is holding a goal out there. I'm giving you the vision that living this way is possible and that there is a real-world example to prove it.

It is possible to dive down deep enough, into the waters of you, where you trust life so completely, where you are able to effectively access your inner peace, that you can be unharmed and unaffected (physically and emotionally) by what is happening around you. You can be so immersed in the world of beauty that surrounds you under the surface that what seems to so greatly affect others roars right over your head. That is the power of riding the wave!

MY JOURNEY: SLOWING DOWN MY EMOTIONS

Because it is only in the times when our emotions are cresting that we can practice this skill of slowing down our emotions I decided to be grateful for the many opportunities I had to practice and since I had three young children life gave me many opportunities to practice.

Although I had begun taking better care of myself and allowing others to help me, which probably alleviated 50% of my reacting, the house was still frequently a mess. In those times I learned to step back, slow down and handle things in a calmer manner. Was yelling really going to help the situation? Was reacting and controlling going to calm my waves of emotions and create the peaceful life I so desired? I still wanted a clean house, but I knew the way I was going about it wasn't working.

At this point I started to realize that there is more than one way to solve a problem, and I wanted above all else to choose the peaceful way. If for no other reason than the fact that I didn't like how it felt when I got angry, I started to yield to peace. Ralph Waldo Emerson says it best: "Nothing can bring you peace but yourself." As I began slowing down on the inside, one avenue that I had control over, I was able to start creating a little bit of peace on the outside, starting with me.

DIVE A LITTLE DEEPER

Now that you have learned how to ride the wave of emotions, by slowing down on the inside, you can easily see that what you are experiencing is bound to pass. Remember the saying, "This too shall pass," as an encouragement, during the times when your emotions are running high. To dive a little deeper under the waters answer the following questions.

• What physical signs do I experience when I feel a wave of emotion coming on? Does my stomach tie in knots? Does blood run to my head? Does my heart begin racing?

• How can I use these signs to step back and slow down?

• What strategies can I see myself utilizing in these moments? Cooling off in another room? Taking a walk? Counting? Be specific so you have a plan!

A WORD OF ENCOURAGEMENT

Towards the end of the book I will give you some tips and daily practices so that you are able to more effectively and easily slow down your emotions, and access that inner peace before the waves come crashing onto your shore which is necessary for you to experience consistent daily peace. Chapter 10 discusses this in great detail. You will have put in some daily training but it can be fun and relaxing. However, at this point, the skill I'd like you to practice is slowing down on the inside for just 90 seconds before reacting. By giving yourself just that short amount of time to reorient you allow your body to physically clear out the chemicals it produced when you were triggered - that is a medical fact. Once they are cleared, you will be back into a non-resistance state and can rationally and realistically start problem solving.

Make peace a priority. As you consistently slow down your emotions and stop reacting to every wind that blows in your life and every wave that comes crashing on your shore, you will find that others will relax and be more peaceful, too.

Because this skill is mastered when you are feeling the emotions crest, you can now welcome them. Notice when you sense your emotions flooding you from within, and practice slowing down and withholding your desire to react. It may take some practice, but soon enough you'll see the effect your slowing down has on the situations and people around you, and you'll be sold out to finding a more peaceful way to live by riding the wave. This completes the second step of the journey: S is for Slow Down Your Emotions.

Chapter 4

What Triggers You?

But you come to a point in your life when you
can't pull the trigger anymore.
— Evel Knievel

When you think of a trigger, what comes to mind? You might think of Trigger, Roy Rogers' famous palomino horse, or a trigger you pull on a gun. If you ever took anatomy and physiology you would probably think of the many trigger points located throughout your body, which is the closest idea to what we will discuss in this chapter.

According to the Merriam-Webster medical dictionary, a trigger point is a sensitive area of the body which, when stimulated, gives rise to a reaction elsewhere in the body. Again, looking at the natural world around us gives us clues to our inner world. Are you getting the picture? Triggers in our body, when touched, cause us to react, to pull away or shout out and typically radiate pain to other areas of the body. Have you ever gotten a massage where the masseuse hit a sore point in your neck which shot pain down into your arm? The same is true when you are triggered emotionally. Something happens on the outside, like children fighting, and it gives rise to a reaction somewhere else in the body, we begin yelling. When someone else hits a sensitive trigger in you, the temptation to react may be great. Don't do it!

MEET THERA

At our home, sitting in the corner of our living room, is Thera, better known as the Thera-Cane. Thera is a personal back massaging device that looks like a weapon. We bought her at a store in our local mall, and she is amazing! If you can, picture a green metal one-inch round rod, about as long as your arm, bent into the shape of a candy cane, and wide enough to fit over your shoulder. She has various round knobs sticking out at odd angles, and she is a trigger point master. If you dig the end of that candy cane into your shoulder blade, watch out!

The best part about the Thera-Cane is you can do it yourself, using the leverage of your own muscles. So why am I telling you about it? Yes, you might benefit from buying one, but the principle of it is amazingly parallel to the idea of recognizing your triggers. When you get your back rubbed by someone else, you may find yourself saying, "A little to the left, okay, over, up, down a little…ah, right there." But you knew where the spot was all along. So the point is that it is your responsibility to find your own triggers and to work them out so they are no longer sore and do not cause you the pain you once experienced from them anymore.

Just like trigger points are focused in a small area yet cause pain to radiate throughout your body, the same is true for emotional triggers. Have you ever noticed that sometimes the littlest things can cause unlikely reactions? This radiates pain outward to those around us. So if this is true, how would you go about releasing your emotional triggers? You can start by simply noticing them. Slow down and become aware that your urge to react is coming from a sore trigger point that is located inside of you and is trying to radiate pain outward. By bringing your attention to the trigger, without reacting to it, you will begin to release the pain.

TRIGGERS ARE DIFFERENT FOR EVERYONE

Another thing to remember is that triggers are different for everyone. Just because you are triggered by a slow driver doesn't mean everyone else is too. This is a very important point to note. If your reactions to situations, events and people are different from someone else's, does that mean your reactions are right and others are wrong? Or does that just mean that people process things in different ways? Seeing that your reaction is not universal will help you bring more objectivity to your perceptions later on in this process.

For example, someone who is scared to death of flying on an airplane will have a completely different experience before boarding than someone who loves flying. It's not the airplane that is the trigger, but the thoughts about the airplane. Noticing this difference is very important.

With children this is a great lesson to teach as well.

Sometimes on the way home from school we have a bit of sibling conflict in the car. Oftentimes it is based on the idea that what someone is doing is not okay and the others want them to stop it. One day Amy was singing a made up song quite loudly and it was not what Molly or Sadie wanted to hear. They were shouting at her to be quiet and telling her how annoying she was being. I calmly said to them, "Amy is simply singing which is completely normal for a four year old. You are the ones who are choosing to be upset. You could choose to sing along with her, to plug your ears, to ignore her or accept that you have a sister who likes to sing. But how you are trying to get her to stop is not okay and it is not going to solve your problem. What do you want to choose?" Although they would have much rather heard me tell Amy to stop singing I wanted them to learn that it was not the stimulus that was causing them to react, it was them. If you don't like how you are feeling choose another response. Don't get trapped into the thinking that it is the outside world that has to change. It is you. Yes, it really is that simple.

If you can remember that thoughts create emotions, you will soon be able to identify your own thoughts that create your negative emotions before they overrun you. This can be a great help in learning to be more objective in life and in breaking free from triggers. Start to accept that how you are reacting is not universal and you could choose another response.

THE SNAKE IN THE BUSH

On the side of my house is a very dense hedge near a brick walkway. It has been cleared out in the middle so that the girls can use it as a secret hide-out. They have set it up quite nicely and have furnished it with a fake fire pit and a little oven with burners drawn on top in Sharpie marker that they made with some left-over pavers. There are countless buckets, shovels, plastic food items and concoctions throughout the area. They have spent hours playing various imaginative games in this bushy area.

Recently a friend came by to pick up her son and upon walking by it commented about what a neat place it was for the kids to play. And then she looked and me and very quietly leaned in and whispered, "Aren't you afraid there are snakes in there?" I had never considered the thought. It never even dawned on me that the possibility of a snake being in there would be something to fear. I looked and her and said, "No."

This hide-out that the girls love so much was, to me, a great kids' play area. But to her it was a snake-infested bush. My thoughts that created my feelings about this spot were drastically different from hers. Neither of us was right or wrong, but each of us created within ourselves the feelings we experienced about this little play area.

WHERE ARE YOUR TRIGGERS?

Identifying your emotional triggers works the same way as trying to find the trigger points on your back. It takes a little trial and error, and a little pushing and prodding, but soon enough you will find them. For this activity I want you to try to identify your triggers and make a list of them. Think of the most recent times when you were angry or frustrated and triggered yourself into a reaction. Did it happen at a certain time of day, when engaging with a certain type of person, or at a certain location? Did you react to certain behaviors or situations? Some examples might be: 5:00 in the afternoon, going to the grocery store, a messy house, financial loss, slow drivers, screaming kids or bad service at a restaurant, just to name a few.

MAKE A LIST OF ALL THE TRIGGERS YOU CAN IDENTIFY WITHIN YOURSELF – THE MORE THINGS ON YOUR LIST, THE BETTER. I'M SURE YOU CAN THINK OF AT LEAST FOUR.

1.

2.

3.

4.

Great! How does it feel to objectively look at this list? I would encourage you to copy this list onto a separate sheet of paper and tape it inside your kitchen cabinet. Then the next time you react to anything, you can bring your awareness to it, analyze it and add it to the list. You can title your list "Master My Triggers" or something silly like that.

Make your list as thorough and detailed as possible so that you know where your triggers are located. This will help bring objectivity when they arise, which is one way you can break free from them. Also, be aware that your list may change over time. Things that trigger you now might not trigger you in the future. Some areas that are not a problem for you now might creep up later. Don't delay. Start your list as best you can, and soon enough you will be familiar with your triggers and won't need to look so diligently.

The more you can add to your list over time, the more accurate and helpful it will be. The triggers you are attached to are a part of the wind that causes the waves of your emotions to fluctuate so dramatically. However, the more you become aware of your triggers, the more you will start to notice when you are allowing the wind to stir up your ocean, and you will see that the trigger, and your emotions will pass, if you will simply allow them to.

This step is pretty short and sweet. Now that you have your list all that is required of you is to slow down and notice your trigger moments, withholding the impulse to react. That's it. Don't react. Don't do anything. Just notice.

MY JOURNEY: NOTICING MY OUTSIDE TRIGGERS

Now that I was making progress taking care of me and slowing down in general, I didn't feel such a persistent underlying tension. I was not as reactive over little things. But the house was still a constant struggle and source of tension. If I had made a trigger list back then, the house would have been number one my list!

One day while I was inside picking up, feeling angry

that it was always me, I noticed that Jim, my husband, was calmly out back reading on the patio, enjoying himself while the girls were playing on the swing set. At that moment an idea came to me. At first I thought it was a selfish thought, "If he is just going to sit out there and read, then so am I!" I stopped what I was doing and, thinking I was being a little rebellious, proceeded to join him with a book. As the kids continued to play in the backyard, I realized that no one cared about the house but me. I just noticed that I was the one being triggered. "Hmm."

DIVE A LITTLE DEEPER

Being triggered by various things on the outside is totally normal. Your job is to simply notice them. Bring your attention and your awareness to these times and see if you can identify patterns. To dive a little deeper under the waters, answer the following questions:

• What patterns do I notice when looking at my list of triggers?

• How do I feel about finding them? Excited, overwhelmed, discouraged.

• If I were to be honest with myself, how does it make me feel to know that most of what I am reacting to comes from inside me because I am allowing myself to be triggered?

A WORD OF ENCOURAGEMENT

When you begin to notice your triggers, don't be surprised if at first you notice them after you have reacted. You might have already yelled at your children, and then a light bulb goes on…trigger moment. When this happens congratulate yourself. This is part of the process. Noticing takes some time. But each time you have that 'aha' moment, the time it takes you to notice your trigger in the future will get shorter and shorter. So take heart and persist, and one day very soon you'll slow down just enough to catch yourself before you react. This completes the third step of the journey: T is for Triggers on the Outside, People and Situations.

Chapter 5

Look Under the Rug

Always write angry letters to your enemies. Never mail them.
— James Fallows

Jane walks into the grocery and notices Susan in the produce section. She hasn't talked to her since she found out that she was spreading rumors about her when she was going through a rough divorce. How could she have been so cruel? She thought Susan was a friend, but obviously she wasn't. A friend would be there in your time of need, and she certainly wasn't.

Olivia has noticed her negative feelings towards Jeremy building up for years now. She finds herself snapping at him over the littlest things — socks left on the floor, leaving the lights on and not helping as much as she thinks he should. She knows these issues are petty but can't seem to stop her anger from boiling over regularly. Why?

What do Jane and Olivia have in common? They both have unresolved past emotional experiences that are affecting their present moment reality and emotions.

STOP LIVING IN THE PAST

"Tim always does that. He is so thoughtless."

"Jodi never learns from her mistakes. I can't possibly forgive her again."

"Jenny did that before, and I'm sure she'll do it again."

All of these statements base their present moment perception on past experiences. How often do we do this? Many times the reason we react is because we can't forget the past and we haven't done our part to forgive. This is another roadblock to living in the present and handling what is before us without attachment to the past. One way to free yourself from this prison is to take a step of faith and forgive.

I'd like to clarify that forgiveness has nothing to do with the other party. It is not something you have to decide with anyone else. Forgiving is done for your own benefit, to release you from past negativity and, as the Bible describes it, so you can be at peace with all people as far as it concerns you.

DO I NEED TO FORGIVE?

You may be wondering if you need to forgive. I have provided a simple checklist to help you decide if you need to forgive. Slow down for a minute and think of someone you may hold unforgiveness towards ask yourself the following questions:

1. Do I feel a pit in my stomach if this person is around or if their name is brought up in conversation?

2. Do I try to avoid this person?

3. Am I not able to find anything good to say about them?

4. Do I react negatively towards this person on a regular basis?

5. Am I frequently reacting disproportionately to seemingly minor things?

6. Do I wish bad things would happen to another person to teach them a lesson?

If any of these are true for you, take notice. They are red flags that are signaling some underlying unforgiveness. Whether you were wronged by someone years ago or whether you are pretending you are not hurt in a marriage or friendship, dealing with your own unresolved emotions is the only way you will be able to restore peace in your life. Don't stuff them back down again because they will resurface.

If you have identified that this is the case for you, it is in your best interest to start the process of forgiving today! The best way to start is to make a list of all the emotions that you feel when thinking about this person or situation. Do you feel angry? Upset? Wronged? Hurt?

Betrayed? What feelings have you ignored or denied? After you do this, start writing about the first one on the list and the events that caused this feeling. You can write a letter to the person or people involved telling them what they did wrong and how angry you were. This is not a one-shot process. You must revisit the same emotion and the same scenario each day, writing and allowing yourself to feel the emotions you have denied until now. As you do so you will find the pain starts to disappear. And one day the pain will no longer be there. You can then write a letter of forgiveness to them. No need to send it. But as far as it concerns you, you can be at peace with them.

Once you have forgiven them you should make a reasonable decision what step you would like to take next. If you would like to invite them back into your life I recommend having a heart-to-heart conversation and getting it all out on the table. Allow them time to talk and be willing to listen. Extend your gift of forgiveness and don't bring up the incident again in the future. Give time and space for them to heal, too. It is important that both parties agree to forgive if you decide to mend the relationship.

If, however, they are unable to forgive, or if they have not changed the behavior that caused you such pain, you might decide that it is best to let them go. You can do this by simply setting your boundaries in such a way that you do not need to see them, talk to them or interact with them anymore. You don't need to welcome them back into your life to 'prove' you have forgiven them, but truly forgiving means that you can part ways and still wish them well. If their name comes up in conversation or you run into them at a later date there are no bad words spoken or hard feelings harbored, as far as it concerns you.

WHEN YOU READ THE PREVIOUS QUESTIONS, DID A PICTURE OF SOMEONE COME TO MIND? IF SO WRITE THEIR NAME(S) BELOW. THEN TAKE THE NECESSARY STEPS TO BEGIN FORGIVING THEM, STARTING TODAY.

_____

_____

_____

TIME HEALS...NOTHING

Sometimes submerged events come in other forms. I will share a story with you about an event that I submerged for almost ten years and how it affected me.

In the spring of 1996 my father was diagnosed with non-Hodgkin's lymphoma. I was 18. A freshman at Winona State University, I was enjoying running on the cross country and track and field teams. I had a boyfriend, good grades and a lot of friends. To be honest, I didn't have a care in the world. But like the tsunami we talked about in Chapter 3, this diagnosis was shocking. It literally destroyed my world. My dad was only 45 years old. How could this be? Not one to directly deal with things and more prone to the strategy of just 'brushing it off,' I continued living my life. I didn't know this tsunami diagnosis would lead to emotional after-shocks.

However, in the few years that followed, I became heavily involved with a controlling church, ended up dating a controlling and verbally abusive man and lost all sense of myself. I dropped out of college, moved home and decided I was going to be a missionary. Does this all sound crazy? It didn't at the time, but that was my way of dealing with my personal tsunami. I was scrambling to make some sort of order out of disorder. My father had always been my bedrock, my strength in every storm, and now he was being taken away. My life seemed out of control, so I unconsciously put the control back into it in unhealthy ways thinking this would create more stability. This is a natural response for most of us. When things seem out of control, rather than going within, we try to control what is outside of us. If you get only one thing from this entire journey it is that controlling the outside world is not what will bring lasting peace. Always slow down and start from within.

My dad passed away on January 22, 1999 at the age of 48. I adopted the 'brush it off' or 'ignore it and it will go away' attitude, and I simply continued on with my life as I had before. What else could I do? It couldn't be changed, right? Thankfully I made two quality decisions and ended that terrible relationship and re-enrolled at Northeastern Illinois University to complete my bachelor's degree in education. And wonderfully, I met a smart, handsome and loving man named Jim. We were happily married in June of 2001.

However, fast-forward a little bit and I was a mess. In a short span of five years I had three healthy girls. I was a young at-home mother, and nothing seemed to be working in my life. I was angry. I was snapping and yelling at the kids almost daily. I didn't know how to deal with all the responsibility that surrounded me. I was still a child in many ways, but I was raising children now, too.

Through some counseling, I unexpectedly uncovered the unresolved emotional pain I had submerged from my father's passing nearly eight years prior to that. I was finally able to cry about losing him. I saw that I hadn't truly mourned his death and that it was affecting me in my daily interaction. It was way under the surface but was influencing my emotions, and was the reason I had anger surfacing so regularly however unbeknownst to me. So there came a time when I had to resolve this life tsunami that I had not cleaned up the debris from yet. It was as if I was living with devastation – emotional devastation – all around me, that I was constantly tripping over, yet I didn't even recognize it was there.

Maybe this is true for you. Maybe you have experienced a time in your life that was just too difficult to face. It was unexpected, unwarranted and unwanted. You thought time would heal, but it hasn't. You know that in your heart there is more to be done. There are unresolved emotions that have not been properly processed, and it could be part of the reason why you struggle creating peace in your life now. The good news is that you can face them, without fear. Experiencing grief, depression and anger and asking the tough questions in life is part of your journey to peaceful living, if that is what you truly desire.

One strategy that works wonders is – you guessed it – to write about it. Let the pain flow out through your pen or into your keyboard. Each day write more, and as you allow those feelings to rise to the surface, you will also be able to release them. If the pain is too much to bear, please seek the help of a professional who can walk you through these emotions with confidence. At that time in my life I could not have resolved all that I was feeling just through writing alone, and the help of a professional was a wise choice. It may be for you too.

Learn to accept that it is normal to have thoughts that will try to prevent you from forgiving such as, "they don't deserve it," "there's no point in forgiving" or "this doesn't apply to me." If you notice you are thinking any of these, be willing to set them aside, and take a step of faith. This is part of your healing process. It is so important. Releasing unresolved past emotions is critical on your journey to peaceful living.

MY JOURNEY: MY INTERNAL TRIGGERS

In conjunction with my constant reacting stemming from my lack of self-care, my need to please others, and the messy house, I had to recognize and deal with the feelings that I had submerged surrounding the loss of my father ten years prior. Although seemingly unconnected to the messy house, my father's death and my avoidance of the grieving process were causing me to react as well. I first had to forgive God because I had unknowingly held Him responsible for his death. I then had to grieve his loss, too. I also had to resolve the resentment that I had towards Jim that had built up over the years that we had been married. Not looking for it, I found that talking with an old friend who validated my struggles and saw me for who I was as a person felt good and I didn't realize it was causing further damage in my relationship. What I also didn't realize is that I had once again gone outside of me to try to find healing when the real answer was inside of me all along. Once I understood the pain I was causing in my marriage because an emotional boundary had been crossed, Jim and I both had to choose to forgive, and together we were able to restore our marriage.

DIVE A LITTLE DEEPER

Identifying internal triggers can be a bit more challenging. But, if given enough time, they will show themselves to you. Remember, the way to see an internal trigger is by noticing that the way you are reacting to a person or situation is disproportionate to the actual situation at hand. To dive a little deeper under the waters, answer the following questions:

• Make a list of possible events that you have a gut feeling you haven't truly dealt with yet. Some keys to notice are the feelings around them may be shame, guilt, anger, resentment or fear. Could it be abuse, divorce, bankruptcy, abortion or death?

• What are the feelings that come to mind for you? Name them.

- What benefits could come to you if you were able to forgive these events or people? What is the benefit to you?

- How would you feel if you were able to resolve them?

- How do you plan to deal with your submerged emotions?

- You must do something to actively release your submerged emotions. Time does not heal anything. Don't just ignore it; do something.

A WORD OF ENCOURAGEMENT

As we have seen, dealing with internal triggers can be done in a variety of ways. I learned a lot about my own grieving pattern by Googling 'avoiding grieving.' Through my research on grieving I found that I experienced the symptoms of the displacer, where I took my unresolved grief and projected it on others, but there are other ways people avoid grieving, like minimizing it, postponing it, replacing it or creating illness within themselves.

This may be helpful to you, too in your own journey to uncover your internal triggers. Whether you have experienced abuse, rejection, eating disorders or have some things you know you have not resolved in your past gaining more knowledge is always helpful. Through your own research you will find out that you are not alone. You have to have the courage to face them and do your part to forgive. Talk about your feelings, validate your right to feel as you do and acknowledge yourself for taking this step. Whether or not anyone else chooses to do the same, it is still important to your overall healing and your ability to successfully travel this path. Don't wait another day. Do a little research and if you feel it is necessary, find someone who can help you resolve your submerged feelings.

Although dealing with internal triggers can seem scary, it is simply the only way to truly gain more peace. If you are able to admit you have unresolved past emotions, you are in the top 5% of people living. And when you face them, you put yourself up in the top 1% of people who are on their way to experiencing consistent joy and peace in their relationships, their careers and their lives.

By taking these steps and healing those areas of your life that have been ignored or submerged, you will gain new clarity. You'll begin to feel that deep inner peace you never thought possible. Go ahead. The waters aren't as scary as they seem. Take the plunge and release all those feelings that are holding you back from the peace that can be yours. This completes the fourth step of the journey: T is for Triggers on the Inside, Healing Submerged Past Events.

Chapter 6
Cross That Bridge

*And I would argue the second greatest force
in the universe is ownership.*
— Chris Chocola

Who is Chris Chocola? I found this quote when Googling 'ownership,' and I am sitting here laughing, mostly because I am asking this question for my own benefit. To satisfy your curiosity, he is a politician who, according to Wikipedia, is the president of the Club for Growth and a host of other things. What the heck does he have to do with this book? Nothing, but if you're at all curious like I am, you probably had to know the answer in order to continue reading. So go ahead, continue.

Regardless, I love this quote, although probably taken out of context, because I would tend to agree with him. I'd say love is the greatest force, and ownership is a close second. Let's take a look and see why it is such a great force and how, by taking ownership, you can cross the bridge that will change you from powerless victim to powerful life creator. But you have to be willing to step on the suspension bridge of ownership, which will lead you from simply recognizing your triggers to being able to *do* something about them and continue on your journey.

DID I CONTRIBUTE?

When working with clients who don't want to admit they played a role in their drama and are stuck in a pattern of pointing fingers and judging the actions of others, the complaining, analyzing and blaming can be endless. This is where I gently step in and talk about ownership. If you are stuck in this pattern you must come to accept that you are not a victim, you are a contributor. A victim is someone who blames others for their problems, and because others are the main source of their discord, in their opinion, they are also unable to change anything.

Up to this point you have learned how to slow down and noticing your trigger moments, but if this next step, ownership, cannot be achieved, you must throw this book in the garbage can. Do you see why? If you truly believe that you had no role, then you have no power to change your situation and this process will not help you. You will be forever stuck waiting for someone else to change. But if you can consider, for just a minute, that maybe you did have a role in your drama, then go ahead and keep reading.

Ownership, as I am referring to it, is all about accepting responsibility for your own feelings, attitudes and actions. It does not mean that you are to blame, or that what happens is completely your fault. That is probably not the case. However, you can notice your triggers all day long, but if you refuse to admit that you are any part of the problem, you remain powerless.

Going back to Janice, the complaining wife, and Matt, her consistently late husband, in Chapter 1, what was Janice's role in her own drama? Maybe she was always nagging. Maybe she was unfaithful. Maybe she was treating him like a child. In working with clients who are stuck in this line of thinking, I as ask them, "If someone had a 5% role in your situation, what might that role be?" Then if they can see even a small way they contributed, I would excitedly encourage them, "YES! Now, can you find another way you contributed?" We'd start to make a list of all the thoughts, actions and attitudes that they could find which in some way exacerbated or created the situation. The more they can find their role, the more power they have to change their world. Can you see that? You only have the power to change you. But the less you admit you had a role or if you are unwilling to accept any responsibility, you will remain an angry, resentful victim.

As part of my own pattern of reacting, I can see that much of it was a combination of all the previous steps. But especially in my relationship with Jim, I had not taken any ownership over my own life choices, and due to the stress of raising 3 little girls, I was projecting that anger onto him. Yet, I chose to have children. I chose to be an at-home mother. I chose to put myself last. I chose to make it my life's work to make everyone else happy. I was the one who did not take a break. Yet, I was allowing myself to become resentful of Jim's apparent freedom, which took its toll on our relationship.

I was jealous that he was able to drive alone, have a lunch break and did I mention drive alone?! Yes, I was that desperate! I looked at other women who didn't have the same life situation as I did – maybe they had grown children or no children – and I would resent them and all the 'free time' they had. See how this left me powerless? I could not do a thing to create change based on any of those thoughts. I was so focused on what others had or didn't have, what others were able to do or did not have to do, that I was not able to enjoy my life and accept the choices I had made. These thoughts plagued me constantly. And because thoughts produce emotions, you can guess the emotions that followed these thoughts were not helping me achieve peace at all. I was unable to see that I had chosen my life.

I remember one conversation I had that was maddening at the time. I was upset that someone wasn't more available or interested to help me with the girls, and I told them so. Their rebuttal was, "You chose your life, and I chose mine." Those words stung so deeply, but looking back they were right. I did choose my life. And others have chosen theirs. The more I was able to focus on my own choices, accept responsibility for them and allow others to take ownership over their lives, the happier and more peaceful I became.

Look at the diagram below and see how your beliefs and actions are currently tipping the scale.

Powerless		**Powerful**
Blaming Others		Accepting Responsibility

HOW DID YOU CONTRIBUTE?

Think of a recent event in which you were triggered into a negative reaction. Maybe you yelled at your spouse or your child, or threw a fit when you didn't get your way. I'm sure you didn't do that, but I had to put that in there for someone else, like you, who is reading this book and may have reacted in those ways. Can you see your role? Slow down, think back to that moment and see what you did to contribute to the drama. Were you impatient? Were you rushed? Were you being inflexible?

We all contribute to the trigger moments in our life in subtle ways: We don't listen, we act in passive-aggressive ways, we cop an attitude, we ignore, we criticize, we judge, we belittle, yet we confuse our actions with what we think others are doing to us. We are quick to notice when someone isn't listening to us, but can we recognize that maybe there are times when we are the one who isn't listening? Take a minute and think about the roles you play most often and see if you can identify them. Look at what you think others are doing to you and see if you can turn it around and realize that sometimes you are actually the one doing it to them.

WHAT ARE SOME WAYS THAT YOU CONTRIBUTE TO YOUR OWN DRAMA? SEE IF YOU CAN IDENTIFY THE ROLES YOU PLAY. FIND AT LEAST TWO.

1.

2.

This is also a great skill to teach children. I use it with my girls all the time. When they come running to me and say, "She hit me." I ask them, "What did you do?" Then the real story emerges. It gives the tattletale child a chance to own up to their role. Most altercations with kids (and adults too) are not completely unprovoked. Usually both children (or adults) contributed. In this way, the child who was hit is not treated as the victim, and the 'hitter' as the bully. Both are held responsible for the ways they contributed to the disagreement, and a resolution can be achieved. Look at these times, especially with sibling rivalry, as a chance to lay the ground work for them to admit they had a role and accept responsibility for it. What a great skill to teach!

Are you feeling more powerful? I hope so! Now that you can see how you are contributing, you can start to change or eliminate your role. It takes two to tango, so decide to shut off that terrible music, walk off the dance floor and quit the dance.

EMOTIONAL OWNERSHIP

Refer back to the list of statements on page 6 and see how they might be changed to help you take ownership. If you turn the list around, it can crack open the door and help you accept a bit of responsibility where you might not have been able to do so before. I have changed the statements to reflect an attitude of ownership rather than victimhood. Compare the two lists and see how different they sound!

*"I am choosing to be mad. I could choose
another response instead."*

"No one can make me mad. I am doing that myself."

"I always have a choice."

"Maybe you are not trying to annoy me."

"I don't have to get upset, even if you continue to do that."

*"People aren't thinking about me as
much as I think they are."*

"Who am I to judge what someone else did?"

"There is more in my control than out of my control."

*"I probably could have done something different,
even if I don't know what that is right now."*

I heard a joke that said, "I married Mr. Right. I just didn't know he was Mr. Always Right!" How difficult it is to live with someone who always thinks they are right. Don't be that person. Softening your position to one of ownership, even if just partial ownership, will help you create peace in your relationships and be more understanding because you realize that you weren't 100% right and the other person wasn't 100% wrong.

As I mentioned in Chapter 4 in my story about Amy singing in the car and the responses the other girls had, emotional ownership is a great skill to teach your children. Children (and adults) can be quick to say, "You made me mad." I remind my girls in these moments that they are choosing to be mad. Then I ask them, "How else could you respond?" This is a great way to put them back in the driver's seat and take charge of their feelings. It really is a powerful skill for anyone of any age. Surrender the idea that you are always right, and take some ownership. Only then can you move on to the next step: observation…from the inside out.

MY EXPERIMENT: HOW I TOOK OWNERSHIP

With regards to my need to have a clean house, taking ownership was a turning point for me. I slowly started to notice that I was the one being triggered when the house was is a state of disarray, and everyone else wasn't. Before, my first thought was to motivate everyone else to help pick up in order to pacify my emotions. I would assign jobs and force everyone into action to get the house cleaned up so that I could be at peace. I thought I was right to make them help and that having a clean house was reasonable. It is to a degree, but the degree to which I expected it to be clean was unreasonable.

Finally after more reacting and controlling, and less harmony in our family, I realized it was me. Jim had a saying that he would recite when the house was disorganized: "Sorry, we live here." It irritated me so much at the time because I realized he didn't value my rigid idea of a clean house as much as I did. I realized I was the one who was choosing to be so upset over the house. I was the one who needed it clean so I could relax. So I finally surrendered that I wasn't 100% right and having a clean house wasn't the only way I could live peacefully.

DIVE A LITTLE DEEPER

Ownership is a powerful step to take in creating consistent peace. When you are able to see that it is not 100% another person's fault, you have cracked open the door to change because you can choose to change your role. To dive a little deeper under the waters answer the following questions:

• Who do I most regularly get upset with? My spouse? My children? My boss? A friend? What is it that they do that most upsets me?

• Can I identify any attitudes or actions that I have contributed to the problem? Even if only 5%? Am I overbearing? Do I nag? Am I passive-aggressive? Am I so over-booked and hurried that others can't keep up with me? Am I too opinionated?

• What are the benefits of taking greater steps of ownership? How does the scale tip favorably my direction the more responsibility I accept?

A WORD OF ENCOURAGEMENT

I want you to focus on the word en-courage-ment. It takes a lot of courage to admit you had a role, and this is often the biggest challenge for my clients. It's easy to notice what others have done. But asking the tough question – what have I done? – is not as easy. Many people stay in denial and don't want to admit they played any role. By doing so they are resigning themselves to a life of frustration, anger and powerlessness. But that is not you! Taking that leap, crossing that bridge and accepting responsibility is such a powerful way to create the change in life that you so desire. Don't let pride hold you back either. It is another stumbling block. Pride and denial are two sides of the same coin.

If you are stuck, and truly cannot see any role you played you can still to cross the bridge of ownership. For those times when you truly didn't play any role read on to see how shifting from judgment to acceptance can aid you on your journey. And I would again en-courage you to really break free from pride and denial. They are not your friends, and they will prevent you from going where you truly desire to go, down the journey to a peaceful life. This completes the first half of Ownership. Read on for another way to cross the bridge.

Chapter 7

From Judgment to Acceptance

*I believe it is possible for two objective individuals to look at
the same "evidence" and come to very different conclusions.*
— *Dr. Ben Carson in Take the Risk*

Dr. Ben Carson is a world-famous neurosurgeon. In his
book *Take the Risk* he goes through a very specific decision-
making process on how he assesses risk, specifically related
to whether or not he will attempt to separate conjoined
twins. The surgery can be life-threatening, so the stakes
are high. Taking all his medical knowledge into consideration, the patients' health conditions and the likeliness
of success, he decides whether to proceed with the surgery
or not, sometimes contrary to what his colleagues believe
to be true. Does that mean he is wrong and the others
are right? Obviously the doctors involved are all highly
trained and specialized, so it would be foolish to think that
either party is acting irrationally or recklessly. The idea that
two objective individuals can looks at the same evidence
and come to different conclusions is often overlooked. It is
quite possible that this may be where you are running into

a stalemate in your relationships sometimes, too. Perception is subjective, even in the face of scientific evidence. So I'd like to discuss how to overcome this hurdle by shifting from judgment to acceptance.

RELEASING THE NEED TO JUDGE

What do you do if you feel you are justified in your reactions? Maybe you didn't have an ideal childhood, or your business has failed, or your spouse left you for someone else, or you lost your house and you can't figure out why all this has happened. You may be thinking, "This is a nice idea for someone else, but things are too bad for me right now. I am angry and I can't help it. I don't see how I played a role in any of this mess."

Let me tell you a story that might shed some light on your situation. This ancient Zen tale holds some secret wisdom that will help you cross the bridge of ownership without figuring out your role and may bring a new peace surrounding the situations you are facing right now.

"Once upon a time there was an old farmer who had worked his crops for many years. One day his horse ran away. Upon hearing the news, his neighbors came to visit. "Such bad luck," they said sympathetically.

"Maybe," the farmer replied.

The next morning the horse returned, bringing with it three other wild horses. "How wonderful," the neighbors exclaimed.

"Maybe," replied the old man.

The following day, his son tried to ride one of the untamed horses, was thrown and broke his leg. The neighbors again came to offer their sympathy on his misfortune.

"Maybe," answered the farmer.

The day after, military officials came to the village to draft young men into the army. Seeing that the son's leg was broken, they passed him by. The neighbors congratulated the farmer on how well things had turned out.

"Maybe," said the farmer.

Maybe. What a powerful word. As a parent I often say 'maybe' to my girls when they ask me for something. 'Maybe,' keeps them open to the possibility when I don't know exactly what is going to happen. What if we gave ourselves permission to say 'maybe' to life a little bit more? What if, like the farmer, we adopted this 'maybe' attitude through all of life's twists and turns? It sure feels better to think positively, trust life and remain open, doesn't it? Saying 'maybe' is soft and flexible. After all you don't know what is coming next.

Often the biggest challenges in life present the biggest opportunities to grow and change. Had I not hit rock bottom I might never have gone to counseling, been able to recreate a beautiful marriage, gotten certified as a Life Coach or be writing this book right now. But when I was on the verge of a divorce, I certainly did not think of it as the biggest opportunity of my life. I didn't know in that moment how it would all turn out. But in hind sight, it did.

If you can acknowledge that you don't know for certain what the future holds, you can relax and forget about trying to figure out all of the details of how life is going to 'fix' your problems. You will be able to steady your emotions by welcoming the present moment, and it will welcome you back. Focus on doing each day what you know to do. Judging everything as either 'good' or 'bad' will keep you on the reacting rollercoaster. Start to look at things with an attitude of acceptance and have confidence that life is wise and is on your side. Release the need to judge and replace your ideas of the 'good' and 'bad' with 'maybe.' You'll find things do work out, even though it might not seem so likely from your vantage point right now.

THINK OF A TIME WHEN SOMETHING 'BAD' HAPPENED TO YOU. WHAT 'GOOD' RESULTS CAME FROM IT? FILL IT IN BELOW.

I CAN SEE AT LEAST TWO POSITIVE OUTCOMES FROM THAT EVENT, AND THEY ARE:

1.

2.

Slowing down and noticing how things from your past have worked out can help you learn to trust life in the present. If challenging situations worked out before, sometimes even miraculously you might notice, they can and will work out again…but will you trust the process of life or kick and scream the entire way?

When I was 19 I bought my first car, a used Volkswagen Cabriolet convertible, for $5,000. It was white with red interior and had a cute black stripe on the side. I loved that car. It wasn't perfect, but it was perfect for me. One day I was driving across town when another car raced out of a residential area, ran a stop sign and pulled out right in front of me. Crash! I T-boned that car and my little VW was totaled. No one sustained any injuries, and after a few weeks of driving around in a rental car I called the insurance company and to find out the status of my claim. I said to the claims representative, "I am fine and I need to buy a new car, so tell me what I need to do." He kindly said, "We can offer you $7,500." Wow! That was a large sum of money for a 19 year old. I signed off and they sent me the check in the mail. With the money I was able to buy a nicer, white Honda Civic del Sol with a removable hard top. It was the cutest little 2-seater you can imagine. I paid for the car, and had a friend drive me home in it because I didn't know how to drive a stick shift! That afternoon I learned how to drive it and to this day I am still glad I know how to drive a stick shift.

Look back at the exercise you just completed. If something 'good' came out of something 'bad' in the past, why can't it happen again? I am sure you can probably think of even more than one event that turned out that way. Keep in mind as you start to release judgment of your current situation that to cross the bridge of ownership peacefully, you only need to accept the moment as it is and keep moving forward. Release the idea that things are inherently good or bad and replace it with an attitude of neutrality. The more you do this the more you will be steady in your emotions like the farmer was. By saying 'maybe' you will begin to go below the surface of the waves and experience the calmness that is always present within you.

DO YOU REALLY KNOW?

"I know they did that to hurt me."

"The store clerks are always rude. It's probably because they hate their jobs."

"Why are people always against me?"

Amanda woke up late. She hardly slept at all last night after getting the word that her mother had been diagnosed with breast cancer. Quickly showering and putting on her red shirt, she rushed off to the local department store where she is a checker. Clocking in just two minutes late her manager shows no mercy and writes her up for tardiness, after telling her that Jill called in sick and they would be one checker short this morning. The store was unusually busy, and being short staffed, Amanda's line was unusually long.

Tina, a young mom with twin toddlers, is at the end of her line. She is frazzled from an hour of shopping with them. By the time she reaches the front of the line ten minutes later, she has had it. What do you think is about to happen?

Do we really know why people do what they do? If Amanda were to be short with Tina because her kids were screaming during the check-out, could she be blamed? If Tina were a bit rude with Amanda for having to wait so long, would she be wrong? But neither Tina nor Amanda knows what has happened to the other person prior to this moment. This is how it is in life sometimes.

If it has taken us this long to notice the patterns of our own reactivity, is it possible to know what someone else is thinking or why they do what they do? No. Is it possible that their reactions have nothing to do with us? Yes. This form of judgment – judgment of others –will prevent us from taking ownership because we feel the other person is wrong without realizing we don't have the whole story. I am not suggesting that you have to associate or put up with unacceptable types of behavior, but when you take owner-ship over your reactivity towards others, without trying to force them to change to make you happy, you can decide what is a reasonable for you to do.

Greg drinks every night. Sarah is tired of his lack of attention and sees his behavior is ruining his relationships, his career and his health. In times past she would have yelled, criticized and blamed, but not anymore. By shift-ing from judgment to acceptance, Sarah can allow him to take ownership for his behavior. She doesn't have to take it personally anymore. She doesn't have to judge him, try to reform him or feel that it is her fault. She doesn't have to understand why he is doing it.

But Sarah understands that she has the power to choose her own responses, and she decides to slow down and ride the wave of her emotions without reacting. She notices that she is the one being triggered by his behavior and also realizes she harbors a lot of resentment towards Greg that is unresolved. She decides to get counseling to resolve some of this pent up anger. Then she courageously takes ownership for her previous attitudes and the pain she has contributed to the relationship.

Although Sarah sees that she did play a role in the damage of her relationship, she is not the one drinking. Greg is. So how can she rectify this? First, she can stop judging Greg and choose accept him as a person despite his behavior. However, she doesn't need to put up with it, and that is also her choice. But she can confidently make that decision without her emotions getting the best of her. In Chapter 9 we will talk about what Sarah might do. Stay tuned for the conclusion of her story.

MIS-PERCEPTIONS

I'd like to share with you two very common yet eye-opening stories of mis-perception from my own life to show you how my mind jumped to completely untrue conclusions in a split second without even trying! I hope that by sharing them you will see that it is quite possible that you have had these experiences too, whether you recognized them or not.

One sunny afternoon I was pulling out of the Target parking lot in a hurry. There was a three-way stop to exit the shopping mall which was busy with cars in every direction. Because I was being impatient, I tried to glide through and almost cut someone off. Thankfully I noticed at the last second, stopped my car abruptly, gave an apologetic wave and yielded the right of way to a white SUV.

I was glad to have recognized my error and rectified it. But now the white SUV, which I so kindly waved at, was in front of me going at a snail's pace. I thought, "They are doing this on purpose to prove a point to me that I was going too fast." Then an arm came out the window and I thought, "I'm not going to be triggered by your anger." I drove a bit further, and they beeped their horn at me. I was feeling a little self-righteous because I was doing everything I could to remain calm and return kindness, even though the urge to beep my horn was present. At least I knew that my trigger was coming from inside of me, unlike this bozo.

I turned off at the next intersection and that car continued on their way. I couldn't help but think, "Gosh, that person needs to get a grip." Suddenly my cell phone rang and it was my cousin, a welcomed reprieve from this lunacy. "Hey, was that you behind me?" she asked. "I was just waving and beeping at you and you didn't notice me. You almost cut me off." We were both laughing…me, because I realized how wrong I was, and her, because she realized I had no idea it was her. I considered how often events like these happen where we judge a situation at lightning speed, never find the real answer, and go on thinking we were 'right' and someone else was 'wrong.' Then we go about telling others our side of the story for the rest of the day. "Can you believe how rude that white SUV was when I was kind enough to let them go…this world is getting crazier every day… people need to get a grip…"

On another occasion I went out for a run with our dog Barkley. I left the house just before Jim was leaving for work so I stuck the house key in my shorts pocket and went on my way. As I was jogging Jim pulled up behind me very cautiously, and he rolled down his window. Another runner was approaching and crossed onto the other side of the road to avoid interfering with the scene: me, the dog, the slow car and the conversation. Jim wanted to make sure I wasn't locked out and then proceeded on to work. I continued on with my run and half way around the circle I saw the same runner. He looked at me and said, "Are you okay? Was that man yelling at you?" I smiled and said between breaths, "No, that was my husband just making sure I had a key." We parted ways and I thought to myself, "Wow, he was running that whole way thinking what a jerk that driver was when that was not even close to what happened." Releasing judgment is one of the best ways to steady your emotions.

MY JOURNEY:
RELEASING JUDGMENT

During my earlier years of being a mother, there were many times that I felt resentful based on mis-perceptions like these. Being home with three children under the age of five was way more difficult and exhausting than I had anticipated. I hadn't exactly 'planned' my life this way. Although I was able to take ownership of my reacting, I still struggled with was being able to sympathize with women who: a) didn't have children, b) had a lot of help with their children, c) seemed to be able to take better care of themselves than I did or d) had more time for themselves than I did. I resented them. I thought that I was the only one who was as busy as me. "How could they possibly understand my life? I never have a spare moment to myself," I often thought.

But when I was able to shift from judgment to acceptance, I came to the realization that I have no idea what their lives are like. I don't know the struggles they face and I never would. My life was simply different. So I decided to be more grateful for the life I had chosen rather than being jealous, envious or resentful of others that I thought had it easier or who didn't understand my life. Instead of feeling trapped, I considered my options. What were they doing so well that I could start doing for myself? I made a choice to take better care of me. I released my need to judge other women and instead celebrated them for who they were and applauded the great job they were doing in managing their own lives. I stopped thinking I knew that someone else had it easier and started accepting my life, as I had chosen it.

DIVE A LITTLE DEEPER

Looking back at your list of triggers, maybe there were certain ones that you were not able to see that you contributed. But if there is no ownership on your part, you will be stuck in a frustrated and powerless cycle of reacting. Shifting from judgment to acceptance is the tool you need to move forward without anger, resentment or frustration. To dive a little deeper under the waters, answer the following questions:

• How do I feel about the possibility of trying to accept what I cannot change?

• What would prevent me from taking steps to release judgment? Can I overcome these hurdles?

• What would life be like if others stopped judging you and criticizing you? How can you do the same for others? Remember you must be the one to first sow the seeds of peace.

• What words would you use to describe someone who allows life to happen, who is non-judgmental and who can accept you for who you are? Can you think of anyone you know or any leader who exemplifies these traits?

• What benefits can you see that could come to you and to the relationships you have if you were to live this way?

• What spiritual exercises, quotes, books or communities might help you on this path?

A WORD OF ENCOURAGEMENT

Using the word 'maybe' leaves the door open for other possibilities. You aren't saying that you are entirely wrong, but you are open to the chance that there is another explanation. You are also surrendering to the idea that you don't know what is going to happen next. 'Maybe' is a powerful word that can keep you flexible and open.

Moving from judgment to acceptance will help you

cross the bridge of ownership if you are not able to identify how you played a role. If you can notice your trigger moments, but you feel justified in your position, or you feel that you are right and the other person is wrong, you will not be able to transform. If that is where you feel stuck, take a step of faith, focus on releasing judgment and you will find that you will become more humble and compassionate towards others. Congratulations! This completes the fifth step of the journey: Ownership. Whether you played a role or need to move from judgment to acceptance you can cross the bridge.

Chapter 8

Looking Within

I shall try to correct errors when shown to be errors,
and I shall adopt new views so fast as
they shall appear to be new views.
— Abraham Lincoln

Our front yard has always been a constant battleground. Living in Florida, the St. Augustine grass is coarse and thick, but is beautifully green and hardy. There is also a weed grass that breeds here quite aggressively called Bermuda grass. It weaves its way into the St. Augustine and is very hard to get rid of. Over the ten years we have lived in this home, the Bermuda grass has overtaken our yard!

Last summer we decided it was time to get rid of it for good. We hired a landscape company to come and rip out our entire yard and re-sod it with St. Augustine. The morning of the grass installation was fascinating. Out came two workers with a sod-cutting machine that ripped the old grass right out of the ground in long strips, exposing the dirt beneath it. They simply had to roll up the old grass and throw it onto their truck. Next a large flatbed truck arrived with palates of rectangular sod pieces. In a matter of hours they had the whole yard laid with the new sod and they were gone. It looked stunning.

Fast forward one year and can you guess what has sprouted again? Yes. That Bermuda grass has grown back with a vengeance. You can see the weeds are slowly killing off the rest of the yard. What happened? We had the old grass ripped out, for goodness' sake! Ah, but you see, they didn't get the roots. The landscapers did a thorough job using a sod cutter to get all the surface cleared out but didn't dig down deep enough.

WHAT AM I LOOKING FOR?

Just like laying good grass on top of dirt that holds weedy roots is pointless, eventually the root cause of our reacting will kill off the peace we thought we laid if we don't dig deep enough to uproot it. It is only a matter of time. If we get stuck dealing with life on the surface level, by trying to control the outside world and the people in it, we will have limited peace. Sure when things go our way all will be well, but eventually the problem will reappear. Consider this: Is your lack of peace due to the problems you face or is it due to your faulty perceptions? Observing your thoughts in the moments you are triggered is the only way you can start to pull out the weedy roots that have taken hold in your mind

Observing yourself before you respond to the situation with a solution might seem somewhat backwards. Typically you feel upset and then take action by trying to rectify life through controlling it, changing it or resisting it. You skip all the steps that would require internal change because you mistakenly think that the change that needs to happen is outside of you. But when you do this you are only ripping out the old grass and laying new sod. You are not digging deep enough to remove the roots that infected the yard to begin with.

Now there are many times when things do need to be changed in the world, and taking action is necessary. However, life can be changed more quickly and effectively and permanently if you first slow down your emotions, notice you are being triggered, take ownership for your role and then see *why* you are feeling the way you are feeling. This is what observation on the inside is all about: figuring out *why* and then surrendering the root cause of that weedy thought pattern for a more peaceable one.

All of these weedy thoughts create disharmony, and if your goal is more peace, I would kindly suggest you consider observing yourself when you are being triggered and seeing if any of these apply to you. If you are frequently experiencing disharmony in your relationships I guarantee at least one applies to you. Here are six of the most common reasons anyone reacts.

One reason we react, which has been covered in prior chapters, is that we are *mistakenly blaming someone else for our feelings*. If you have ever said, "You made me mad," this category applies to you. I love to remind my girls when they are upset that no one can make them mad. They are choosing to be mad. The same goes for someone making you happy, proud, annoyed, frustrated, nervous or angry. Just eliminate the phrase, "You are making me..." from your vocabulary and you'll be better for it.

The flip side of the same coin is when *we make a situation about us when it really isn't*. Assuming someone did something to intentionally make you mad is ridiculous. People aren't thinking about you half as much as you think they are. The phrase I would suggest also eliminating that ties into this is, "Can you believe so-and-so did…" Trust me they weren't thinking about you when they did what they did, and even if they were, you still have the power to choose whatever response you want. So lay that one to rest.

The second and often the most typical reason we react is because *the way things are right now is not the way we think things ought to be*. Or, put another way, we wish things were different than they are. This is a conclusion we often jump to unconsciously. We think that if things were different they would be better, and since they are not how we hoped they would be, we cannot accept life as it is. For example, let's say there is too much traffic on the road and we are already running late. We typically might feel anxiety rising up in us as we dart in and out of the lanes trying to find the quickest route. We are more likely to get angry at the slow driver who won't get out of our way. Why are we feeling like this? Because we are not able to accept that we are stuck in traffic and we are going to be late. This is not what we want to happen or what we had planned, so we resist it. This applies in any situation and in any relationship in which our ideas of how we think things should be is different than the way they are.

The third reason we react is because *we think we are above what is happening*. Sure this thing could happen to other people, but not me. For some this could be hard to admit because it is a direct blow to your ego. But that is good! That is exactly what we want. Consider the at-home mother who was a successful professional in years past. She is now relegated to changing diapers, cooking meals and doing laundry. She longs for the days of hearing praise from her co-workers on a job well done. She finds that she is frequently frustrated over the little things. Sure she loves her baby, but she feels it is beneath her to be doing all this grunt work and can't seem to find the joy in it. Another common way this mindset is triggered is with financial loss. Especially as we get older and feel we have worked hard, done our best and given to others, it can be very difficult to experience a business failure, a home being foreclosed on or take a big hit in the stock market. Feeling we are above what is happening will keep us stuck in an angry reactive pattern.

How do you feel when your spouse acts in embarrassing ways at a social event? What about when your kids are being bratty at the grocery store? What about when your boss questions the way you handled a work-related problem? If you get angry in these situations it is because *your sense of self is feeling diminished by someone else's behavior and/or you are upset because someone questioned your authority.* Simply put, we don't like to feel embarrassed, be questioned or have our authority challenged. It all comes down to wanting to be viewed favorably in everyone else's eyes at all times and when someone does something to jeopardize our feeling of being in control, having it all together or looking good, we don't like it, and that causes us to react.

The fifth weedy pattern is *thinking and acting out of rigid standards.* Maybe you have already noticed that this is one that I struggled with in regards to my need for a clean house? I was unable to see that my inflexibility was causing me to get upset. I didn't see that having a messy house was okay too. Maybe you can identify with this one. When you think something has to be a certain way or else you get upset, this applies to you. If you view the world as black and white, if you are inflexible and unable to see that there may be other ways of doing things (or other valid opinions), this probably applies to you. There is no shame in admitting it. Just notice that it is the reason why you are often reacting. If the kids aren't sitting at the dinner table as nicely as you think they should, maybe you are being too rigid. Kids are kids; fidgeting is normal. If your schedule is set and it gets changed and you are unable to 'go with the flow,' that is a red flag that you are being too rigid. In kindergarten my daughter Molly struggled with crying and was frequently anxious over changes in the daily schedule. She was being very inflexible. I can remember her teacher saying "This is what we plan to do, but it could change." See, everything we need to know we did learn in kindergarten! Being flexible with life is a great way to create peace.

Finally we get to this last reason which can sum up all the prior ones together: *thinking you are right and someone else (or some situation) is wrong.* Wow. Do I need to elaborate on that? Think of the last time you were upset. I bet in some way it was because you were really convinced you were right. Because you thought you were right you were unable to listen to what someone else had to say. You were just waiting for your turn to prove your point. You didn't really hear them or try to understand them. Why would you waste your time doing that when you know you are right? Many relationships end on this note. There are irreconcilable differences often stemming from the inability each has to consider another's point of view. Why do we get so upset with our children at times? Because we feel we are the parent and we are right. How sad. This mindset causes division and disharmony. How can anyone feel secure, loved, valued and accepted when they don't feel heard or validated in their opinions, feelings and decisions? Slowing down, listening to what someone has to say, and allowing them to explain why they did something or didn't do something is a great way to build a partnership with your spouse, your child or co-worker. Stop judging others and just accept that they are doing the best they can with the knowledge they have. Allow others the freedom to make mistakes without it making you upset. If we truly value peace, like we say we do, then surrender the idea that you are right. As the saying goes, "It is better to have peace than to be right." But is it to you?

NOW WHAT?

Hopefully you can see at least one root cause of your reacting, and now comes the fun part. You can learn how to grab hold of it and pull it out. Remember riding the wave of our emotions before responding is the goal, so here is what you do in that moment. Slow down. Breathe. Notice you are being triggered and search for the root thought that is causing you to feel upset. Maybe you notice you are passing judgment on the situation. Maybe you are wishing things were different than they are. Maybe you are being too inflexible. Step back and see what category your weedy thought fits in and then uproot it.

Are you upset because your child is questioning your authority? Surrender. Is there a more peaceable way to parent? Can you slow down and consider your child's needs and opinions rather than viewing your role as a parent as a complete dictatorship? Can you respect that they are individuals and are entitled to their opinion and maybe if you took a moment to find out what they had to say, together you could solve the problem peacefully? Begin by responding in a way that better supports your higher goal for peace.

Are you yelling at your spouse because there is not enough money to pay the mortgage this month? Are you jealous of those around you that seem to be able to afford things you can't? Can you slow down and notice that your feelings are stemming from the root that this shouldn't be happening to you? Can you accept that this is how it is right now and release judgment?

Do you see that the common solution is to slow down and accept? Allow your feelings space to kick and scream inside of you if you must, and then detach from the emotions, without reacting, and identify the root cause. Each time you choose not to react based on these thought patterns, the roots will weaken and will soon be replaced by the peace seeds you have sown which will grow peace all around you.

Surrendering and accepting is not weak. It is very powerful. Nothing was ever solved through anger. Lasting, fair and concrete solutions can be found only when we take our emotions out of it. There is nothing to fear in doing this and everything to gain. Imagine the problems you could solve with a stable frame of mind. Imagine the relationships you could build and cultivate if you could simply bring people on board with you through peace rather than driving them away in anger. Yes, life can be consistently peaceful and calm when you make the decision to create it that way from the inside out.

Review the following list of weed seed thoughts. These ways of thinking are what habitually cause you to react. This is where you really get to look underneath the surface and have the opportunity to be honest with yourself. You can identify your own weedy roots and then choose to pull them out.

LOOK BACK TO YOUR LIST OF TRIGGERS IN CHAPTER 3. CIRCLE ANY OF THE FOLLOWING 'WEED SEED' THOUGHTS THAT MAY HAVE CAUSED YOU TO REACT.

1. I thought I was right and someone else was wrong.

2. I was blaming someone else for my feelings.

3. I was making the situation about me when it really wasn't.

4. I thought I was above the situation and it shouldn't have been happening to me.

5. I felt my sense of self being diminished by someone else's behavior.

6. I wished things were different than they were.

7. I was passing judgment on another person or situation.

8. I was acting out of rigid standards.

9. I got upset because someone was questioning my authority.

Noticing the weedy root thought that is causing you pain is where you can start to break free from the urge to react. Let's turn each of these weedy beliefs around and see how your thoughts could look if you were to surrender them for a more peaceable way of thinking. Then you will find you are truly able to create consistent and lasting peace. That is what you want, right?

Here is the list of peace seed thoughts that you can sow in any circumstance. They are written to correlate with the previous weed thought of the same number. Uprooting the weeds is a simple process. All you have to do is choose not to react based on a weed thought, and then choose to plant a peace seed thought in its place. In this way peace will begin to flourish in your life. When faced with a potential conflict situation yield to these peaceful ways of thinking instead.

CIRCLE ANY OF THE FOLLOWING 'PEACE SEED' THOUGHTS THAT MATCH THE NUMBER YOU CIRCLED IN THE PREVIOUS LIST.

1. I know that I am not 100% right. I can listen to what someone else has to say and give weight to their opinion too.

2. I am completely responsible for my feelings right now. No one can make me feel badly, I am choosing that response.

3. I know this situation is not about me. People struggle with their own problems and are not thinking about me as much as I think they are.

4. I can learn from every situation I face. Things can happen to anyone and I can handle anything that comes my way.

5. What other people choose to do does not diminish me as a person. It is not a reflection of me in any way so I don't need to be upset by their behavior.

6. Things are the way they are supposed to be right now and I can accept them. I can look for solutions while moving forward to create more of what I do want.

7. Who am I to judge? I do not know why people do what they do or why certain situations present themselves to me, but I choose to accept rather than resist them. I choose to have compassion for others and to remain humble.

8. I can easily flow with life. I do not need to have things my way all the time to be at peace.

9. It is okay if someone questions me. I am willing to explain my point of view and listen to others. I do not need others to treat me with respect in order to have respect for myself. I do not need to get upset either, but can be clear about what I will tolerate and set my personal boundaries accordingly.

Now the next time you sense a reaction coming on see if you can choose to plant a peace seed rather than react off of a weed seed. Can you see how these ways of thinking lend themselves to peace? Can you feel the shift in thinking that will disarm others? Can you imagine how your relationships would flourish if you were to adopt these new peace seed thoughts? How would it feel to not be on guard anymore, but to be able to consciously and deliberately slow down and uproot weedy thoughts while planting the seeds of peace in their place? Remember that facing conflict is your opportunity to uproot a weedy root and plant a peace seed in its place and when you do you will see that peace begins to blossom in your life.

MY JOURNEY: OBSERVING ON THE INSIDE

Observing on the inside and seeing all the ways I was attached to these disharmonious thought patterns was eye-opening for me. When I look back now I can clearly see that most of the weedy thoughts listed above applied to me! I can see that I was attached to a rigid idea of how my house 'should' be. I thought that it was unacceptable to have a messy house, even though I had three children at home with me. I was wishing things were different than they were. I didn't want to live in all this chaos and clearly resisted it. I was blaming my feelings on someone else (or, in this case, the messy house). I can remember saying to Jim, "It's like my feelings are tied to the state of the house. If the house is clean I'm happy and if it's not I'm mad. " Up until now I tried to control my environment in order to control my emotions and it was a losing battle.

Then I finally realized I could break free from my rigid ideas and get off the emotional rollercoaster I was riding. I was able to see that there was more than one way to live. I started accepting that sometimes the house may be messy and that it was alright. No one was going to die if the dishes didn't get done at night or the laundry was still piled in the basket. I stopped allowing the state of the house to influence my feelings of self-worth. I stopped passing judgment on myself as a person. I stopped controlling others and enforcing them to create the rigidly clean house I desired. Peace slowly started arising within me and spreading to the world outside of me.

DIVE A LITTLE DEEPER

Like the example of my weedy grass you can choose to uproot your own weedy thought patterns and plant peaceful seeds instead which will sprout with time. The goal here is to expose the root reasons why you are reacting, and surrender them, thereby bringing awareness to the patterns you are repeating which are creating the disharmony you are experiencing in your life. To dive a little deeper under the waters, answer the following questions:

• Upon looking back over the reasons why you are triggered, which seemed to apply most often to you?

- Why do you think so?

- Write about a time when you reacted, and specifically identify the patterns that were in play during that situation.

- What is the purpose of recognizing these root causes of reacting, and how can you slow down and observe them?

A WORD OF ENCOURAGEMENT

Maybe like me you can see that a few of these weedy thought patterns are deeply rooted reasons why you consistently react. Slowing down and bringing awareness to them is all it takes to start uprooting them. The next time you react see if you can identify the root cause from the list provided. Be deliberate in your efforts at first, and over time you will become more familiar with these weeds and you'll see how they spread into many areas. For me, being rigid not only affected the way I managed my house, but spread into the way I parented my children, how I viewed religion and into my overall personality which was quite opinionated. This is likely to be true for you too. So if you notice one weed thought follow the root around and see if is spreading into multiple areas of your life. When you are finally able to completely uproot the pattern that most influences you and causes you the most conflict, you will find inner peace. Congratulations! This completes the sixth step of the journey: O is for Observation on the Inside.

Chapter 9

Be a Fly on the Wall

I am turned into a sort of machine for observing
facts and grinding out conclusions.
– Charles Darwin

Typically, jumping in to the ring and putting on your verbal boxing gloves is the first step if you are in an angry state of mind. You observe what is happening and boom, you strike. But in our journey to peaceful living, taking action on the outside is actually step number seven! First you have to slow down your schedule and your emotions, then you have to notice your external and internal trigger and take ownership for your feelings. After that you start to observe the weedy root cause for your reacting and start to dig it out. Now you can detach from the situation and begin to observe it objectively. That is what I call being a fly on the wall. So how does one go about observing situations objectively?

First imagine the scene unfolding before you as if you weren't a part of it. Look at what is going on in the third person. For example, the fly might see a scene like this: A mom is upset because her children are fighting. What might the mother do? Depersonalize it as a bystander would with no emotional attachment to the outcome. There are a few guidelines to help you effectively evaluate any situation as a master problem solver.

IS THIS SITUATION **H.O.T.**?

One important thing to consider when you are observing any situation and the people in it is to assess whether or not the situation is H.O.T. What I mean by that is to consider if anyone is:

Hungry

Or

Tired

I remember long ago discovering that doing things when I was hungry or tired was pointless. Let me explain. One night after dinner I was busy making lunches for the next day and getting the girls in bed when I came out to the kitchen and saw the dinner dishes were still out everywhere. I was exhausted from a long day and felt utterly defeated. Normally I would have gotten upset and frustrated and forced myself to clean up, but that night I didn't have it in me. I collapsed and went to bed, and when I awoke, I noticed it wasn't that bad. There were literally only five or six dishes there. Why had I felt so overwhelmed the night before? Like the world was coming to an end? Because I was tired! Lesson learned.

As you have heard, part of my struggle was that I was rigidly attached to the idea that the sink had to be clean before I went to bed. See how difficult we make life for ourselves when we are unable to be flexible. But that night, unknowingly, I chose peace for myself. What a blessing it was.

In parenting this strategy is especially helpful. When your children are acting up consider whether it is possible that they are just hungry or tired? Sometimes the best solution is simply popping a bag of popcorn and putting on a movie for them. Many times, before I learned to slow down my own schedule, I would find that by 4:00 my girls were very disagreeable after I had dragged them around all day. Not recognizing this, I thought they were being disrespectful so the disciplining and fighting would begin. If I would have known about this technique, first I would have realized the reason I was being triggered was because someone was questioning my authority. But then I could have stepped back, detached from that root and said, "What might a mother do whose children are acting up at the end of a long and busy day?" Then I would assess if part of the chaos was due to the fact that they were hungry or tired. If so, there was the solution.

If your spouse is being disagreeable ask yourself, "Are they hungry or tired right now?" If so, the best choice is to address the real problem. Don't bring up an intense conversation. Make a meal or allow for a rest period. But as far as it concerns you, there is no reason to get emotionally stirred up about it. An objective logical solution will do. I'm sure you get the point by now. Address basic needs first.

WHEN THE SITUATION IS NOT **H.O.T.**

Jim, my husband, has been a member of the Bonita

Springs Rotary Club for almost 15 years. If you are not familiar with it, Rotary was founded in 1905 and is one of the world's largest not-for-profit service organizations. The thing I love best about Rotary is its 4-way test which shows how people from all walks of life, from different nations and religions, both women and men, can problem solve together and come to solutions that serve all of humanity. For over 100 years this code of ethics has been recited by the club members at all weekly meetings. I believe we can find peace in all situations if we can answer these four questions in the affirmative. Taken directly from the Rotary International website the 4-way test is as follows:

Of the things we think, say and do
1) Is it the truth?
2) Is it fair to all concerned?
3) Will it build goodwill and better friendships?
4) Will it be beneficial to all concerned?

Can you see how using this line of questioning can help you resolve all conflicts fairly and peaceably? What if you adopted this 4-way test in your life? It would make for a lot more peace and objectivity, wouldn't it? Yes, if you search for an answer in this manner, you will find the peace you are seeking.

When the moment is not H.O.T. you can use these four questions to help you find solutions that are agreeable to all parties involved. Ultimately every situation is factual, not good or bad, and if we look at things from a neutral perspective, solutions are easier to find. Every problem has an answer if you are open and flexible and can be reasonable and realistic. Because you have given yourself the chance to break free from the root cause of your reacting, you are no longer emotionally wrapped up in your own inner dialogue and will be better able to listen to others and thoughtfully consider their ideas.

WHAT CAN SARAH DO?

Remember Sarah and Greg from Chapter 7? Greg is still drinking, and Sarah is sick of it. She knows that yelling doesn't work. She knows that criticizing doesn't work. She has tried cajoling, encouraging, pestering, nagging and talking to him, all with no effect. What can Sarah do?

By the time she gets to this stage of her personal journey to peaceful living, it is time to for Sarah to start utilizing the strategy of third-person questioning to come up with a solution which will create space for her to think from another point of view and to see objectively. Sarah can ask herself, "What might a wife do when her husband drinks too much every night?" By answering this question, she can come up with ideas that could work. She doesn't need to pick one yet, just consider as many solutions as possible, listing them all. If she were making a list, it could look like this:

- ◻ I could join a support group like Al-Anon.
- ◻ I could do some internet research.
- ◻ I could set boundaries for myself and decide what I will tolerate from here on out.

◻   I could ask a friend for advice or help.

◻   I could talk to a professional counselor.

◻   I could choose to leave.

Writing out a list of possible solutions is a great starting place, especially when considering what to do on more major issues. Of course, in your day-to-day interactions, this will not always be possible or necessary, but certainly looking at a written list can often help to clarify what solution is best. Now Sarah can consider the questions above applying them to her current situation.

1) Is it the truth that Greg is drinking too much? Yes.

2) Is it fair to her? No.

3) Does it build goodwill and better friendships? No.

4) Is it beneficial to all concerned? No.

By doing this she can see that what is going on right now is not healthy. So what solution could she choose that might help her regain balance in her life? What is a reasonable step? Being objective means that whatever she chooses does not need to be done out of anger. It is done as a way to bring a solution to a long-standing problem.

At this point Sarah can look at all the options that are available from her list and then pick the one that feels right to her, again considering the questions above as a guide to her decision-making. Starting with Option 1 Sarah can apply the questions which might sound like this:

1) Does joining a support group like al-anon offer truthful solutions? Yes. Al-anon is a long standing support group for friends and family of problem drinkers.

2) Is it fair to all concerned? Yes. It would only help me find solutions and be able to better help Greg.

3) Will it build goodwill and better friendships? Yes. I would most likely meet others who can offer me support, and it will help heal my relationship with Greg, too.

4) Will it be beneficial to all concerned? Yes. I would get the help I desperately need, and there is nothing unfair about doing that.

Sarah can run through this line of questioning with each of the options she wrote and by doing so will find the best, most logical and most peaceful answer for her life that takes Greg into consideration as well. It may reveal some solutions that are not reasonable because they do not pass the four-way test and those can be eliminated.

Try this the next time you are in a pickle. Write out a list of possible solutions and run each one through the four-way test. Teach this strategy to your children. Post it in the kitchen on the refrigerator and help your children problem solve using these four questions. Use it in the workplace. Teach your employees how to utilize it to solve their own problems before coming to you. You will be amazed how effectively others are able to come up with solutions, resolve conflicts and create peace in their lives too.

MY EXPERIMENT:
OBSERVING ON THE OUTSIDE

Now that I could see that I was attached to a rigid idea of how my house should look along with some of the many other patterns I was attached to, what did I do next? This was when I began to detach from my feelings about a messy house and look at it objectively. I started to say, "What might someone do whose house is messy?" "What possible actions might that person take?"

Thinking back my list might have looked something like this:

- ¤   If I am hungry or tired I could take care of that first.
- ¤   I would only focus on the house if I was in a positive state of mind.
- ¤   I could relax my standards a little bit.
- ¤   I could pick up one area and leave the rest.
- ¤   I could completely ignore it and go have fun.

Then I would take each possible solution on the list and run it through the 4-way test. A whole new world started opening up to me as I realized that the way I was reacting wasn't specific to the situation, it was only specific to me. Some days I fell back into my old rigid patterns, but at this point I started to let go. I found freedom from my emotions and started to relax and look for peace even when the house was a mess. I also realized how hard I had been on myself for not being perfect. I slowly became more accepting of my flaws and didn't hold a stick over my head if the house wasn't perfect. I was able to detach and decide what was reasonable for me to do or not do when the house was in a state of disarray.

Finally, I was able to enjoy life, not because the house was always clean, but because I surrendered my rigid ideas of how my house should look. I could engage in messy projects with my girls without thinking about the mess we were creating. I began to accept my life, with three young children, as it was, without needing it to be different and without feeling that my house was a direct reflection of me as a person.

DIVE A LITTLE DEEPER

Being a fly on the wall can be quite interesting. Looking at life from up above gives a different perspective. To dive a little deeper under the waters, answer the following questions:

- Describe the benefits of being a fly on the wall. Do you feel this approach could help you? Why or why not?

- Describe in detail the things a 'fly' would or would not think and how they would or would not act as an observer

- In what ways specifically does this action or non-action create peace in the observer and in the situation?

- What concrete reminder can you create to help

you remember to observe before acting? Hint: Maybe you can make a fly and tape it on your refrigerator.

A WORD OF ENCOURAGEMENT

If you have made it this far and you are still reading, congratulations. Being objective and looking at situations in the third person is a great way to solve life's many problems. Detaching and depersonalizing will give you the objectivity you need to be able to be a non-reactive problem solver. It will help you appropriately assess each situation and then consider all possible solutions. You will be able to include the input of others and find a peaceful solution that is agreeable and reasonable to all. This completes the seventh step of the journey: O is for Observation on the Outside.

BEFORE YOU GO ON, CHECK IN WITH YOURSELF. HOW DO YOU FEEL SO FAR? TAP INTO YOUR INNER DIALOGUE AND SEE IF THIS IS RESONATING WITH YOU. WHAT CHALLENGES DO YOU SEE ON THIS JOURNEY? WHAT BENEFITS ARE YOU EXCITED ABOUT? WHAT QUESTIONS DO YOU HAVE? TAKE A MINUTE TO DO A GUT CHECK AND WRITE YOUR ANSWERS BELOW.

Chapter 10

Keep the Momentum Going

I try to learn from the past, but I plan for the future by focusing exclusively on the present. That's where the fun is.
— *Donald Trump*

The concept called Presence, the last on our journey, is nothing more than doing what Mr. Trump does: focusing exclusively on the present. It's not a strange idea. Most religions encourage focusing on the present and not worrying about tomorrow. In the Bible, Jesus exhorts the people, saying, "Do not worry about tomorrow, for tomorrow will worry about itself." But how many of us do it?

Worry impedes us from enjoying the present because it keeps our focus on the future. Regret also hinders us because it keeps our focus on the past. Can either of these be changed by focusing on them? This moment, right now, is all we have. So why not decide to enjoy it?

You may wonder how you can enjoy life when you have so much on your mind. This is where the practice of presence comes in. Just like exercising is a life-long strategy for physical health, not just an activity to lose weight or achieve a goal, practicing presence is simply the journey we take, each day, to train our minds to connect with now. It is not a short term fix. To start you have to make a decision that following Mr. Trump's advice is beneficial.

LIST 3 EMOTIONAL, PHYSICAL, SPIRITUAL OR OTHER BENEFITS OF PRACTICING PRESENCE IN MY LIFE.

1.

2.

3.

Allowing your focus to be here without judgment, without fear, without wishing for the future or holding on to the past is crucial to your overall journey to peaceful living. To be able to do this consistently is rare for most people, but you are different! By practicing presence you will be able to teach yourself to love what is, in whatever form it comes. You will learn to how to access the deep inner peace that is always present inside of you through accepting life, without wishing it were different. Remember, you are the great and peaceful ocean whose waters are always calm beneath the surface, no matter what is roaring up above.

EXERCISES TO INCREASE PRESENCE

We have touched on a few of the strategies to bring presence into your life already. Forgiveness is one of them. By forgiving anyone and anything we release ourselves from emotions that are tying us to the past. This is so important. We can also exercise our muscle of presence through acceptance, denying the impulse to judge, allowing life and embracing the word 'maybe.' By acknowledging the fact that you don't know how everything will turn out, you can be at peace knowing that life is not against you, it supports you. By releasing anger, resentment, frustration, judgment and discord you will start increasing presence in your life.

To tie this all together I'd like to revisit the analogies we made in Chapter 3. Remember that you are the ocean, vast and deep and peaceful and your emotions are the waves on the surface. This is the part of the journey where we learn how to dive below the surface even deeper to access our inner peace, to go under the waves, and find safety from life's storms. Do you recall Faye and Eugene, the couple who rode out the Sumatra tsunami while scuba diving without even realizing it? What other analogy can we draw from their example?

Knowing that the physical realm of life, if you're perceptive enough, is a mirror image of the spiritual realm how does the physical act of scuba diving reflect into your spiritual journey for deeper peace? When you scuba dive, metaphorically speaking, on this journey you go below the surface of your emotions through the exercise of meditation. Fran and Eugene were taking time to explore the quiet beauty that lives in the ocean. You can do this too, by quieting your mind and exploring the beauty you have within you. It is very simple, but because it is a new concept to many it can seem intimidating. It doesn't need to be though. Meditation is simply relaxing, being still and watching your thoughts. You are not trying to control them, or stop them, but you are becoming the observer of them. Through meditation you will see that within you there is always peace, regardless of what is roaring up above.

Although there are many forms of meditation, I recommend starting out with the breath meditation. To do this all you need to do is focus on your breath. That's it. Start by picturing a feather on the end of your nose and breathe in and out so gently that it does not float off. Try to make your exhale as long and slow as possible. Allow your attention to remain on your breath, and your thoughts and feelings to pass by in the background while you watch each one as it forms and floats away. For the beginner, meditation is most easily started with a guided CD or program. When I started practicing I downloaded an app on my phone called Mindfulness Meditation, which I still have and use on occasion. It doesn't really matter what you choose. Just do it.

RIGHT NOW, CLOSE YOUR EYES AND TAKE 1 MINUTE TO FOCUS ON YOUR BREATH. THE GOAL IS NOT TO ACHIEVE A STATE WITHOUT THOUGHT BUT TO ALLOW THE THOUGHTS TO COME AND GO AS THEY WILL WHILE YOU ARE FOCUSING ONLY ON YOUR BREATH. IT IS PERFECTLY NORMAL IF YOUR MIND WANDERS OFF. WHEN YOU NOTICE, GENTLY BRING IT BACK TO THE SENSATION OF THE BREATH GOING IN AND OUT OF YOUR NOSTRILS.

How did it feel? Were you able to overcome your resistance and allow one minute to pass without doing something? Or did you just skip the exercise and continue reading? If so, go back and do it. I know it seems nonsensical, but it works. The more you slow down and practice this exercise, the easier it will be to bring presence into your daily interactions with others too.

There is one more piece to the Sumatra Tsunami story that I'd like to share. Upon being interviewed by CNN after their miraculous survival the newscaster asked Faye and Eugene to describe what they experienced. They said they noticed the water visibility worsened and they felt like they were being sucked down.

HERE IS AN EXPERIMENT YOU CAN TRY AT HOME. ALL YOU NEED IS A GLASS OF WATER AND SOME SAND. POUR SOME SAND INTO THE GLASS OF WATER, COVER THE TOP AND SHAKE IT UP. WHAT HAPPENS TO THE WATER WHEN IT IS SHAKEN? WHAT HAPPENS WHEN IT IS CALMLY PLACED BACK ON THE COUNTER AND LET TO SIT?

Many times, whether through a larger life tsunami or simply from being too busy our ocean is shaken and life can get very cloudy. Maybe you feel that at times, like answers are hard to come by and you feel quite foggy. By sitting quietly and stilling your mind, you allow the sand to settle on the bottom of your ocean, which will bring inner clarity. Meditation is the way to do this. It will suck you down deeper below the surface if you allow it to. Make time every day to just sit and be still. Visualize the sand settling on the bottom of your ocean and allow clarity to rise within you.

It is quite interesting to see what comes in and out of your consciousness when you are not even 'trying' to think anything. Meditation is not a religious practice, but can be incorporated into any spiritual path with success. How can slowing down and watching your thoughts cause harm? It can't. Even Jesus encouraged us to, "Be still." So go ahead and try it. Over time you will see that it is not *you* thinking but your mind on automatic pilot which is creating a lot of the incessant internal chatter you previously thought was you.

Another strategy that is quite fun to try is to picture the voice in your head as a person sitting in the seat next to you while you are driving. Listen to the endless negative chatter and non-stop talking. Give that person a name, imagine what they look like and notice their flamboyant mannerisms. Would you put up with that criticizing, judgment and negativity from a friend? No way! How long would it be before you told them to shut up and kicked them to the curb? Then don't allow your mind to do that to you either. Reign it back in and direct it to the types of conversations that you want to have.

A word of caution: Don't be fooled by the thoughts that say:

"This doesn't work,"

"I don't know how to do it,"

"This isn't for me" or

"This is just dumb. I'm going to skip this section."

It is normal to have resistance, but don't allow it to stop you from trying something new. I often have to encourage clients to quiet these thoughts when trying anything new. If you don't try something different, how are you going to get different results? What have you got to lose? Make a commitment that for the next 30 days you are going to focus on your breath (see, you don't even have to call it meditation) once a day for at least 1 minute.

EXERCISES TO INCREASE PRESENCE:

FORGIVENESS
ACCEPTANCE
NON-JUDGMENT
ALLOWING
"MAYBE"
MEDITATION
SLOWING DOWN

MY EXPERIMENT: CULTIVATING PRESENCE IN MY LIFE

Despite my own initial resistance (yes, I face resistance, too), I learned how to meditate. Through the use of the meditation app on my phone I began to exercise my weak muscles and learned how to focus more of my thoughts and energy in the present moment.

I started looking forward to the times when I had 5 minutes in the car alone. Instead of flipping radio channels, I would shut it off and be still. I also started using the 10-minute relaxation recording before I went to bed at night. After a short while I noticed that I was more aware of what I was thinking. I could see how my thoughts were running wild at times without my consent. I started to choose what thoughts I did and did not want to listen to and was able to see it as only the 'thinker' in my head. I realized that I did not have to accept every thought that came to mind but could choose to think and feel however I wanted. Over time I learned how to focus on my breath without the aid of the meditation track.

To this day, focusing on my breath is a skill that I frequently use when I am feeling upset. I detach from what is going on that is upsetting me and immediately focus on my breath. This begins my 90-seconds-to-peace journey and gives me the opportunity to slow down, notice my triggers, take ownership, observe my weedy thoughts and then come up with an objective solution. It is a process, an exercise that I play around with, experiment with and enjoy. It is something that brings me peace in all of life's many storms.

DIVE A LITTLE DEEPER

In order to build your muscle of presence so you can experience lasting peace and move past the urge to react, you must begin a daily practice of meditation. You have to decide what works best for you and create a workable plan that you know you can stick with. To dive a little deeper under the waters, answer the following questions.

- Write your own definition of presence.

- List three benefits of exercising your muscles of presence daily. How would it make you grow or change in positive ways?

- Review all the possible ways you could exercise your muscles of presence, as listed above. Can you think of any others? List them.

- Circle the two that seem most relevant to you. Would you like to learn to meditate? Do you want to make a regular practice of journaling? What about yoga or walking? What about finding a positive group, in your community or online, that you can be a part of?

- How do you plan to incorporate these two things into your daily schedule? Who will be of help to you?

A WORD OF ENCOURAGEMENT

Living in the present moment is as foreign to most of us as speaking Chinese. It takes practice, just like learning a new language would. You can start as I did with practicing meditation. Start in small the moments when you are not triggered. If you are at home in the morning drinking coffee, take a moment to look at it. Smell it. Examine the mug it is in. Really taste it. If you are exercising, take off your headphones. Listen to the sounds around you. Feel your heart beating. Sense the touch of your feet as they move across the ground. Look for the birds up in the trees. When you are lying in bed at night before you doze off, notice your breath. Feel the weight of your body on the mattress. Relax your muscles and just watch your thoughts move in and out of your consciousness. These simple exercises will strengthen your muscle of presence so that when you are triggered you will be strong enough to ride the wave, dive below the surface and find the peace that this present moment has to offer you. Congratulations! This completes the eighth step of the journey: P is for Presence starting on the inside.

Chapter 11

Resist or Allow?

The point of power is always in the present moment.
— Louise Hay

Be here, accept now. That is presence. In this final step of our journey, bringing presence to the outside, we translate the internal presence we practiced in the previous step and allow it to flow out of us. By doing this we will be grounded in the present moment. That is the entire goal, if it could be simplified to such a degree as this. Life is lived in this moment, and now is the only moment that matters. Can you see how this all ties in together? The whole purpose of our journey is to help us release our ideas of how things should be, how we wish they were or how, if they were different than they are now, things would be better. It is helping us to become aware that when we are reacting based on our judgments of the past or our fear of the future, we miss what is going on now. Detaching from those feelings and reactions, even if only for a moment, will help us to start living here, now, with peace.

REACTING VS. RESPONDING

I am sure you have heard of this comparison before, but it is truly what makes our journey to so powerful. When we react we resist the present moment. We are in effect telling ourselves and the world, "This is not okay with me, and I am going to kick and scream unless things change!" When we respond we embrace the present moment in whatever form it takes and use it to change our perception. We use our trigger moments to bring us into a state of presence so we can objectively see what is going on before us. Only then can we effectively come up with a solution that is agreeable to all.

Let's think of it in this way:
Reacting = Resisting
Responding = Accepting

I'll share one last story with you about Barkley, our 80-pound ball of fur and friendliness, who loves to bark and play. Most of our neighbors know him, and certainly their dogs do. One afternoon I was in the front of our home sweeping the entry when a woman walked by on the road. Barkley, in his good-natured way, wanted to go out and greet her. He bounded out to the street, the way happy dogs do, and gave a light-hearted bark. He wanted to play. She immediately went into a resistance mode, raised her arms up and started shouting, "NO! NO!" to which Barkley returned the resistance. Instead of seeing her as a friendly neighbor, he now saw her as a threat. He mirrored back her fear and began barking more loudly at her. She assumed Barkley was mean and acted off of this assumption. However, had she greeted him with a welcome pet, she would have had a completely different experience. Needless to say, I ran out, grabbed Barkley, apologized profusely and calmly encouraged her to put her arms down.

Assume Barkley is the present moment. He is friendly. He wants to play and be loved. But when you are scared, when you put your arms in the air and shout 'no,' he will return that fear back to you. That is why it is always best to greet a dog with your hands at your side and allow them to sniff the back of your hand. By doing so you are welcoming the dog into your space. The same is true with the present moment. If you shout and resist, the present has no choice but to mirror that same resistance back to you. But when you welcome it kindly, with confidence, knowing it is only there to greet you it will return your kindness.

BE FRIENDLY WITH THE PRESENT MOMENT

Sheila is excited because tonight is the night she is hosting a dinner party in her new home. She sent out the custom invitations a few weeks ago, and seven of her closest girlfriends are going to join her this evening for a fabulous Greek dinner, recipes compliments of Barefoot Contessa. As she starts cooking she notices her cat throwing up on the carpet in the front room. Keeping her spirits up, Sheila calmly goes and cleans it up. "Oh, well, no one will notice that little spot," she thinks. While she is cleaning it up, the spinach pie burns. "Crap," she musters. Meanwhile the leg of lamb that is sitting on her grill is getting overcooked, and she realizes she forgot to buy the pita bread. Her internal temperature is rising. And before she can rescue the lamb from the grill the doorbell rings. Her first guest has arrived.

Sheila has a choice: She can resist this moment, get frustrated that things aren't going as she had planned and be less than welcoming to her friend when she answers the door, or she can accept this moment as it is. She can release the idea that things need to be perfect and welcome her guest with a smile and warm hug. What will she choose?

The present moment is your friend waiting outside the door to your party. How will you choose to answer the door? Frustrated? Angry? Irritated? Wishing they would go away? Or will you be able to answer the door with a smile and welcome this moment? Can you make this moment a friend rather than resist it as if it were your enemy?

There is only ever one way that life is lived, in the present moment. Did you know your relationship with the present moment can bring you the success you hope for or can, in the end, defeat you? It all depends on how you view it.

THE ILLUSION OF FUTURE HAPPINESS

"Once the kids are out of diapers,
it will be easier."

"Once this event is over,
my life will slow down a bit."

"I'll be able to relax
when I get this project done."

"I will be happier, less-stressed, relieved when..."

Do any of these sound familiar? Although they seem like they are filled with hope for more peace in the future, they prevent us from being happy now. Going back to what I told you about my experience in the foreword, getting stuck in a state of when this happens, then I can be happy, is a certain trap. All these statements make our happiness depend on some arbitrary, future event that usually never comes. Living in the future is another hindrance to bringing presence on the outside.

Once the kids are out of diapers, suddenly they are talking and fighting more. Once we get that charity event behind us, we are asked to be the chair for another event. Once we finish our project at month's end – poof – a new one hits our desk. There is no when. The future never comes because, just like magic, when it arrives it only takes the form of the present moment. Did you ever think about that? Right now you are living the moment that years ago you thought was in the future. Yet, here you are. It is now. Release the idea that you can't be peaceful, you can't relax and you can't enjoy life until something else happens first. Decide to make friends with the present moment and see how things start to look differently than they did before.

BRING PRESENCE INTO YOUR WORLD

The more you can bring presence into your world – being here, now, without attachment to the past or fearing the future – the more power you will have to meet the challenges you face with a positive solution. Bringing presence each day to the moments when you are feeling triggered concludes the final step of your journey.

First you slowed down both on the outside and on the inside, noticed your triggers and took ownership by acknowledging your role. You learned to accept rather than judge; then you learned how to observe yourself and then the effectively assess the situation through outside observation. Finally, without crashing into your emotional waves, you were able to navigate below the surface, scuba diving to find the peace that resides inside of you and then bring it to the present moment to impact the world around you.

You now have all the tools you need to be able to come up with a solution that is beneficial to all concerned. You can live at peace with what is and you can create peace wherever you go. Congratulations – you have successfully learned to ride the wave and have completed your unique journey to peaceful living.

MY EXPERIMENT: BRINGING IN PRESENCE EACH DAY

As I said in the beginning of the book riding the wave is not a quick fix, but it will give you ultimate freedom from reacting because the focus is on changing you, not the outside world. Once you are familiar with these steps though, you can navigate the waves of your emotions and find peace in just 90 seconds. That is a promise. Here is what my journey looks like when I'm feeling upset.

Starting with focusing on my breath, I walk myself through each step. I see if I am feeling triggered because I am too busy. I quickly assess whether anyone, including me, is hungry or tired. I see if I am being too rigid in my thinking or if I am unable to accept what is. I take ownership for what I am contributing to the problem. Then I run through the 4-way test and start coming up with solutions by involving those around me (usually my children). Do you see how, by slowing down and focusing on my breath, I can buy myself the 90 seconds I need to quickly run through all the steps of the S.T.O.P. journey? If I am not able to come up with a solution or if I am still feeling triggered and emotionally charged, I do nothing. I have learned that no good will come out of my yelling or anger. So I just let it be.

These days my house is perfect all the time. Yeah,

right! Seriously, not much has changed on the outside. I still have three girls. I am still married to the same man. I still live in the same house, although I'm sure the furniture has been rearranged a few times since I started on my journey. But now I am able to relax more. I don't feel that my house is a reflection of me. I have been able to adopt Jim's attitude of, "Sorry, we live here." Yes, I still like a clean house. But it is not a requirement for me to be happy. I am not resentful anymore either. If I decide to clean up, it is because it is what I am choosing to do. If I don't feel like it, then I won't. I have learned to be flexible with myself and with others.

And now that I have given everyone else the freedom to exist, without the pressure of trying to make me happy by not making messes (which would be an impossible task), they are more likely to help with a glad heart. By giving up control and not seeing it as 'my job' anymore, I have allowed everyone to realize that they are contributing to the mess, and by Sunday night everyone is motivated to get it cleaned up. What a difference!

So you see, the actions taken may not be that different, but what is different is how we get the results we are after. Are we forcing our rigid ideas onto others, or are we surrendering and yielding to a more flexible and peaceable way of life? Being free from reactivity, without the need to control the outside world, is true freedom! And do you know what, magically, most of the time, my house looks pretty good.

DIVE A LITTLE DEEPER

The final step of this journey to peaceful living is learning to live in this moment consistently, without effort. The more you use this route for your journey to peaceful living as shown in Chapter 1 and summarized in the chart provided in Appendix A, the less you will need it. Soon you will be able to ride the wave with ease and dive down into the deep to access the peace that lives in you. To dive a little deeper under the waters, answer the following questions:

- Write for 20 minutes about how life could look if you were able to live with peace, no matter what was going on around you. How would you feel? How would others around you respond to your change? Dream about what you can create simply by changing your approach to life.

- Read back over your writing and see what stuck out for you the most. Write that on a card as an intention and look at it each morning when you wake up. For example: "I have peace of mind at all times and the world around me is a safe, happy and enjoyable place to live." Make sure to phrase your statement in the present, not the future tense. Keep that card in your purse or where you can reflect on it often.

A WORD OF ENCOURAGEMENT

Congratulations! This completes the final step of the journey: P is for Presence on the outside. By building up your muscle of presence first on the inside you will be able to create peace and bring your mind to the present moment so that you can allow life and ride the wave. Now that you have completed the journey, it is just matter of time before you see the results in your life. Remember, your peace depends on you. If you are not experiencing the peace you would like to have, don't look for others to change. Look within you. It's your life, your journey, your wave. Have fun and ride it well!

Chapter 12

From Peace to Happiness

Happiness is the meaning and the purpose of life,
the whole aim and end of human existence.
— Aristotle

Let's get to the real heart of the matter. Maybe throughout this journey to peaceful living, you have taken each step as it was presented. Starting with slowing down your calendar and setting boundaries you were able to eliminate a good portion of the stress and reacting you were habitually facing. You learned how to ride the wave of your emotions and to watch them rise and fall without reacting to them. Then you made a list of triggers on the outside, such as people who cause you to react, certain situations, places and times of day, so that you were able to start noticing where the landmines were for you. Whew! That's a lot already.

But you kept on with the journey and started to dive really deep, deeper than you ever expected, where you uncovered the internal triggers you had submerged over time. Maybe you had to resolve feelings of resentment over a divorce you went through, maybe you had to forgive someone who hurt you, or maybe you had to forgive yourself for past mistakes. Whatever it was, you had to do it, because the journey to peaceful living stops when you are unwilling to uncover and deal with what has been submerged for so long. And how were you able to identify those internal triggers? By noticing the disproportionality with which you react to life at certain times, to certain people and in certain situations. If the reaction doesn't fit the moment, bingo – you hit that internal trigger.

My goodness, if you've stuck with it this far…why not travel a little farther? And you did. Thinking all the hard work was behind you, you then had to cross the bridge of ownership. Admitting you had contributed to the situation is the only way to truly get past the need to react. When you started looking at your trigger moments from this perspective you were able to see the ways you played a role in creating that situation, and you uncovered the real gem called humility.

Knowing that you contributed in some way, to some degree and understanding that reacting will only perpetuate the problem, you were able to slow down even further and look inside of you to see why you are feeling so upset. Were you supposing you were right and someone else was wrong? Were you being too rigid? Were you allowing your self-worth to be tied to someone else's behavior, thereby feeling a need to control that person? Were you wishing life was different than it was? These are just some of the root causes why we all are prone to reacting at times, and you learned that once you can see them for what they are – weedy patterns of thinking – you could choose to uproot them and plant seeds of peace in their place. Finally, you learned how to be a fly on the wall. Through depersonalizing and asking questions in the third person, you were able to objectively come up with fluid responses to meet the needs of all concerned, and you were able to include others in the decision-making process. Wow! What a journey.

To maintain and increase your peace over time you learned about presence. Through the daily exercises you chose, whether journaling, reading spiritual material, participating in a positive group or community, practicing yoga or meditation, or any combination of these you were able to create more peace of mind and harmony with life and with others which in turn increased your ability to remain in the present moment on the outside, not stuck in the past or wishing for the future. No more ups and downs for you! You are able to accept each moment, knowing that life supports you and the way it presents itself is simply an opportunity for you to grow.

Some might argue otherwise, but as I see it, the meaning of life is happiness. You can't live for some future moment. You can prepare for it. You can take steps towards a goal you are trying to reach. But the only moment you have is here before you now. Your life is lived in moments that appear in this space you have before you called the present. Don't you want to be happy now?

The message of true happiness that can be experienced through this journey to peaceful living is that of releasing our illusion that the outside world has to appear in some form that is agreeable to us and then, only then, can we be happy. You can choose to be happy, whatever your situation is right now. You don't have to live your life on a rollercoaster of emotion. You have the power to create the life you want and to let go of the things that don't serve you.

You can choose to make a change, take care of yourself and set your boundaries. That is where it all starts…you taking care of you.

HOW DOES HAPPINESS COME?

But what if you have peace and you still are not happy? Unfortunately, that can be the case. We have discussed at great length the journey to peaceful living, and I'd like to leave you with one final thought. If, as Aristotle says, the point of life is happiness, then how does peace translate to happiness? Other than the idea that mastering your emotions is quite rewarding and is sure to bring you more satisfaction in your relationships, your career, your family and your life, maybe you have a sense that something is still askew. You can be at peace on the inside and on the outside and still be unhappy. If this is the case, there is one last exercise that you can practice as part of your daily presence exercises, and I call it 'Break the Illusion of Happiness.'

MY HAPPINESS CHALLENGE

My children go to school a half hour from where we live. It just so happened that way. It wasn't by design. So for the past five years we have been driving them and picking them up two times a day, an hour round trip. It would be easy to let this rob my happiness. If I consistently complained about the drive, was jealous of others with a shorter commute and hinged my happiness on living closer, I may be waiting a long time!

Now I can say that I would prefer to live closer to school, but I know that moving will not make me happy. If I am unhappy now, that is not an outside problem, it is an inside problem. Instead I have learned to accept this situation and use my time wisely. I have listened to countless audio programs and enjoyed long conversations with my kids. Even in the times when my husband and I have considered moving I remind myself that a move is not going to make me happy. It might be more convenient and time-saving, but I try not to base my decisions on the promise of greater happiness. This goes back to the thought we already covered that tries to trick us into that illusion of happiness, "If I just lived closer to school, then I could be happy." And remember that if I am not happy now, buying a new house closer to school will not bring me the happiness I am looking for.

Have you known someone who moved from job to job to job? There was always a reason why their current job wasn't the right fit…the co-workers were incompetent, the boss was a jerk, the tasks they were asked to do were below them. Then they went in search of another job, worked there for a while and the same excuses surfaced again.

Making changes on the outside will not produce lasting happiness any way you slice it. You can want things. You can desire change. But you don't have to wait to be happy until you get them. This is what breaking the illusion of happiness means. Not waiting for happiness to come through any-thing, but accepting life now and choosing to be happy because you know that nothing on the outside has the power to make you any happier than you are now. It is an illusion.

Embrace the idea that this moment is here, and it doesn't need to be different. You do not have to be attached to anyone or anything. You can make a decision to be happy, even in the face of having circumstances that you would prefer not to have. Yes, you can have relationships you enjoy. Yes, you can drive a nice car. Yes, you can enjoy eating at your favorite restaurant. But the moment your happiness depends on the relationship working out, or the car remaining in pristine condition, or your reservations being made at a certain place, you have given away your ability to remain at peace and unhappiness returns. It is reframing your mind to one of preference, not necessity. Embrace the idea that, "I want you, but I don't need you." "I would like that, but it is not necessary for my happiness."

Write down a time when something happened that robbed you of your happiness. What was it: the loss of a relationship, a job or a home? What illusions were you attached to that caused you to allow yourself to be unhappy? Were you relying on that thing, that person or that situation to fulfill you or to make you happy? Was it the idea that you could not be happy without it? Now that you have gotten past it and found yourself happy again, can you see that going through the unhappiness was actually unnecessary if you had realized at the time that your happiness did not depend on that thing, person or situation?

PARTING WORDS

I realize this is a huge concept to throw at you in closing. But I think it is worthy of presenting because I want you to understand that peace and happiness are your right. You have the ability to create the life you want, starting from the inside. You can break free from the emotional rollercoaster of trying to control the outside world in order to have sustaining peace and happiness. It is really true. If you haven't been able to identify in part because your situation is too difficult or your circumstances seem too unfair I would encourage you to read a few books that describe people overcoming significant hurdles in their lives. It will help you to see how they were able to remain sane, find internal peace and move forward without losing hope. I have personally read and highly recommend:

Left to Tell by Immaculee Illbagiza – In 1994 Immaculee survived the Rwandan genocide despite losing her entire family by living for 91 days hidden in a small bathroom with seven other women. She shows how her faith was deepened during this time of complete devastation.

Breaking Night by Liz Murray- Born in 1980, Liz tells the engaging, descriptive and heart-wrenching story of her poverty-stricken childhood. Raised in a New York City ghetto by drug-addicted parents, Liz's tale is one of survival and ultimately success. Liz overcame these odds and went on to win a New York Times scholarship and admittance to Harvard. In 2004 Liz's story was produced into a made-for-T.V. movie called: "From Homeless to Harvard" and the book was published in 2010.

Even Silence Has an End by Ingrid Betancourt – In 2002 Ingrid, while running for the Colombian presidency, was kidnapped by guerillas and lived for six-and-a-half years in the Amazon jungle. Despite dire circumstances she was able to keep her spirits high and kept hope alive until her ultimate rescue.

You can create happiness, and peace, wherever you are right now. Don't wait another day. Don't wait for anything else to change. It is up to you!

Final Note:

If you are in a dangerous situation or are being abused in any way please seek out professional help and remove yourself from the situation. This should be your first step. Please visit the National Domestic Abuse Hotline www.thehotline.org or call 800-799-SAFE (7233). This service is available in all 50 states, Puerto Rico and the U.S. Virgin Islands.

IT'S YOUR TURN

I have shared my journey with you, and now it's your turn to do the work to create lasting change and enduring peace in your life. Start simply by slowing down. Can you say 'no' to a few activities? Can you begin taking care of you first? Can you stop trying to please everyone else but you? Can you validate your feelings in the process? All of these suggestions are great places to start.

If you haven't already, complete the exercises in this book. Feel free to share your experiences with me as you grow or ask any questions you have on my Facebook page, April's Life Coaching. Don't forget to join our community at apriloleary.com; there's a free gift waiting for you when you do. I'll keep you in the loop with what's going on and how you can join up with us.

If you enjoyed this book and saw yourself in the pages you might want to consider signing up for our Ride the Wave Tele-Course. They are held monthly and will take you step by step through this material in an engaging and transformative way. As long as you have a phone you can participate! For more information, upcoming class schedule and easy online registration go to www.apriloleary.com/ridethewavecourse. When you register for the course you'll also receive the Ride the Wave Workbook free. It is not available for purchase but is a special perk I offer all class participants. Ask a friend to take the class with you. It's a great way to grow together.

I sincerely thank you for joining me on this journey and wish you the greatest, happiest, most fantastic life ever! May your transformation take you on a journey to peaceful living that you never thought possible!

Appendix A

Ride the Wave Chart

On the Outside / On the Inside

S — Slow Down

	On the Outside	On the Inside
MySchedule	Have I overcommitted myself? Have I said 'Yes' when I meant 'No'? Do I need to set tighter boundaries? Am I forgetting to take care of myself?	
My Emotions		Can I ride the wave of emotion right now? Tip: Feel it but don't react. Journaling is always a safe outlet. Know it will pass. Reacting in a state of agitation is never productive.

T — Triggers

	On the Outside	On the Inside
People and Situations	What type of people trigger me? Which situations trigger me? Are there certain times of day that trigger me? *Make a List of Your Triggers so you can become more aware of them.	
Submerged Past Experiences		Am I reacting disproportionately to the situation at hand? Why? Are there unresolved experiences that I have submerged which are resurfacing in other ways? What are they?

O — Ownership (The Bridge)

What is My Role In My Own Drama

On the Outside	On the Inside
What actions did I take that contributed to this drama?	What attitudes and thoughts can I identify that may have contributed to this drama?

Observation

- Look Inside Me First.
- Consider H.O.T.!
- Use the 4-Way Test

On the Inside	On the Outside
What ideas am I attached to? Replace weed seed thoughts with peace seed thoughts.	Be the fly on the wall. Observe with non-judgment. Is someone Hungry Or Tired (including me)? Run through the 4-Way Test to find a solution that is fair to all concerned.

P — Presence

- Be Here, Now.
- Acceptance is the key.

On the Outside	On the Inside
How can I bring my full attention, to this moment? What is stopping me from being here, now?	Reacting = Resisting Responding = Accepting Be friendly with the present moment.